BREAKTHROUGH

BREAKTHROUGH

Conquering Your Creative Demons and Achieving Success

J. Dharma Kelleher

Copyright © *2021* by Dharma Kelleher.

Published by Dark Pariah Press, Phoenix, Arizona.

Cover design: JoAnna Kelleher

All rights reserved. No part of this story may be used or reproduced in any manner whatsoever without written permission from the author except in the case of brief quotations embodied in critical articles or reviews.

Library of Congress Control Number: 2021919309

Paperback ISBN: *978-1-952128-16-5*
Hardcover ISBN: *978-1-952128-17-2*

*To my wonderful wife, Eileen.
You have been my greatest cheerleader.*

Acknowledgements

As this is my first nonfiction book, I have a lot of people to thank for sharing their experience, strength, and wisdom.

Most notably, kaay grosso and all of the women of the Garden Club, an informal group of women that gathered every week for years when I was newly sober. You created a safe space for me to be real. You provided an abundance of food for both body and soul. You held me to account when I struggled and stood with me when I stumbled. I will forever be indebted to you all.

I also want to thank those you showed up to the rooms of Alcoholics Anonymous, Al-Anon, and Codependents Anonymous. I would not be alive if it were not for you.

I want to thank the many other mentors who have shared their wisdom with me over the years including Joanna Penn, Seth Godin, and most recently Chase Jarvis.

Last but not least, I want to thank my amazing wife Eileen for being my best cheerleader. I couldn't have done this without you.

Table of Contents

Acknowledgements	vii
Foreword	xi
Introduction	xv
1. What Is Creative Self-Doubt?	1
2. We All Feel Like Imposters	9
3. Using Meditation to Release Self-Doubt	13
4. Affirmations	21
5. Willing to See Things Differently	25
6. More Tools for Your Toolbox	35
7. Healthy Body, Healthy Mind, Healthy Muse	43
8. Understanding Your Creative Process	51
9. Focus on the Work, Not the Results	63
10. The Middle Way	69
11. The Beginner's Mind	77
12. Rediscovering the Joy of Creation	83
13. The Comparison Delusion	89
14. Dealing with Feedback	97
15. The Delusion of Reviews	103
16. The Delusion of Success	111
17. Shiny Object Syndrome	119
18. Writer's Block	125
19. When the Creative Well Runs Dry	131
20. Dealing with Burnout	137
21. Pay Attention to Self-Talk and Feelings	141
22. Sitting with the Fear and Self-Doubt	147
23. Nonattachment to Your Work	151
24. Dealing with Failures and Flops	157
25. Leveling Up	163
26. There Is No Silver Bullet	167

27. Getting Professional Help	171
28. Changing Course and Walking Away	175
29. Final Thoughts and Parting Shots	179
30. Resources	183
Index	195
About the Author	201

Foreword

Imposter syndrome, *noun*, a psychological condition that is characterized by persistent doubt concerning one's abilities or accomplishments accompanied by the fear of being exposed as a fraud despite evidence of one's ongoing success.
—*Merriam-Webster Dictionary*

I had no intention of starting the foreword with a definition, but after reading this in the Merriam-Webster Dictionary, I had no choice. I've never seen a word so well conveyed.

Most people have experienced imposter syndrome. The executive who gets a big promotion and worries they'll be exposed, once and for all, as incapable of doing his job; the mechanic who frets the cars they repair are running by sheer luck; the attorney who is certain they're going to blow the next case despite being highly respected in their field. It's self-doubt, it's powerful, it's damaging, and it's painful.

It's easy for imposter syndrome to hold one back from accomplishing their goals, but for writers it can be especially difficult because we work alone. We don't have a boss breathing down our neck who we are certain is looking for the smallest excuse to fire us. We are our own boss.

In fact, most of us don't have to do it all. Most writers work traditional full-time jobs which rules out the need to write to keep a roof over our heads and food in our bellies.

Although most writers don't have to write to meet physical needs, we have no choice but to write. Why? Because we're writers. It's a paradox. Writers love to write but hate writing. There are few passionate enough to endure the pain of exercising their passion.

Without my knowledge, a prominent author I highly admired for decades read my book, and then sent me an email to tell me how much he enjoyed it and why. He was kind enough to write a blurb for me. I sent him my second novel, and he loved it just as much.

You would think that would have given me all the confidence I need for the rest of my life. Instead, I focused on knowing other well-respected authors who told me they purchased my book but never mentioned it again.

I am guilty of reading good books and neglecting to drop the authors a note to tell them. Yet when others don't do it for me, I'm devastated. They have validated my work is garbage and I debate if I should continue to bother.

Most self-help books published in abundance through the seventies and eighties were dull. We may have gained insight from their pages, but it was drudgery to get through them. This is especially true of those with graphs to explain why we are who we are, followed by exercises and questions we're expected to fill out to better ourselves.

This book is not that. It qualifies as a self-help book, but hardly a boring one. And thankfully there are no graphs or fill-in-the-blank exercises. It does require you to do three critical things. To have an impact, this book requires the reader to think and do some self-reflection. But most importantly, as J. Dharma Kelleher emphasizes throughout the book, you must be willing.

Criticize and doubt every word if you would like, but at least consider them. Be willing to think to yourself, "I'm not sure these concepts and tools will help, but I'm willing to try them." You may even find not trying them impossible.

The author is persuasive. She is persuasive but kind. She is a drill sergeant on one page and gentle the next. The reasons will be clear to the reader. She vehemently believes in what she teaches, but knows it's not easy. Therefore, she demands the reader do nothing more than try it.

Dharma uses the short list method. If you're unfamiliar with a short list, it's a list of tasks to be completed each day. Typically, the short list is used by people with mental disabilities to assist in completing daily duties. These may be as simple as taking a shower, brushing your teeth, or getting the mail. The beauty of the system is you cannot fail.

If a person is unable to achieve their goals, there is no self-judgement, only an assessment. Acknowledge the goals were too idealistic and make the list shorter the next day. This book teaches a similar method. Not beating yourself by feeling defeated. Acknowledgement, accept, and move forward.

Midway through my second novel, I was overwhelmed with self-doubt. My first novel was well received, but that didn't prevent me from believing it was dreadful. In the moments when I felt confident it was well written, I couldn't move past my misguided belief that writing another novel of equal quality was impossible. That kind of luck happens only once in a lifetime.

In a desperate attempt to move past imposter syndrome, I asked, "When do you reach the point you stop worrying whether you're good enough?"

If you were a successful author, a prolific author, an

author I held high regard, or all the above, you received an email, phone call, or text from me. I didn't like the responses. Not only did they say the same thing, but most also responded with the same words, "I'll tell you when I get there."

J. Dharma Kelleher does not dodge the reality that most writers live with imposter syndrome. She doesn't pretend to have a magic formula or give you tricks to work around these challenges.

You will learn how to look your self-doubt in the eyes and move forward. Accept its existence and keep on writing because keep writing you must. Because you are a writer.

Brad Shreve
Author of the Mitch O'Reilly Mystery Series
Host of the Queer Writers of Crime podcast

Introduction

If you want to skip this introduction, by all means, go for it. Basically, I'm going to explain who this book is for, why I wrote it, and what qualified me to write it. I also share my author journey to date, including many of the challenges and setbacks I've faced. I hope you find this book helps you.

I wrote *Breakthrough* primarily for those of us who write genre fiction—thrillers, fantasy, science fiction, romance, etc. However, if you write literary fiction, nonfiction, poetry, or even sales copy, you will still benefit from the lessons shared here. Creative self-doubt affects most of us regardless of what we write.

If you are a creative person in another medium, such as painting, graphic arts, sculpting, dance, or whatever, you may also get a lot out of this book. You may just need to translate my words to correspond to your specific media.

This book focuses on mindset and our emotional (and, dare I say, spiritual) journey as authors. It's about breaking through the wall of negativity and self-doubt that plagues so many of us. This book is about helping you, not necessarily your bottom line. Changing your mindset may help you sell more books and get bigger advances and more reviews. It may not. But either way, you will enjoy the process a lot more.

So, what qualifies me to write this book?

Let me start by telling you what I am not. I am not a therapist. I don't hold any advanced degrees. I am not a guru or life coach or spiritual advisor or Zen master. Take anything and everything I say with a grain of salt.

As of the time of this writing, I don't make a living with my writing. I'm not a bestseller. I've never won any awards for my writing. Not one. Haven't even been nominated. I don't have an MFA. I'm not one of the cool kids who gets reviewed by the *New York Times* or interviewed by NPR's Terry Gross.

Here's one more thing I am not. I am not a naturally confident person. I have struggled with insecurity since early childhood. Perhaps I was born with it.

I was one of those "sensitive" kids, the ones that bullies like to pick on. And they picked on me a lot. From first grade through my senior year in high school, I had a target painted on my back. I was quiet and introverted. I loved to read and learn, found science and math breathlessly fascinating, and was a natural at language arts. My teachers adored me, which only made my social life worse. No one wants to be the teacher's pet when it means getting shoved into a locker in gym class.

Speaking of gym class, I was not athletic at all. I was the shortest kid in my grade every year. I was a slow runner, couldn't throw or hit a baseball, and was the one always picked last for teams.

On top of all of this, I am transgender and in a same-sex marriage. I've dealt with abuse, bullying, and discrimination my entire life. I share this not to elicit your pity but to make a point.

I understand what it's like to live with self-doubt. I know what it means to look at everyone else and feel like a fraud and a mistake. My mother was fond of saying, "You have so much potential. Why don't you use it?" No matter what I did, it was never good enough.

I struggled with depression and trauma for much of my teens and twenties. Beginning my gender transition helped tremendously in some respects, but it also brought more abuse, harassment, and trauma into my life. I became an alcoholic and codependent, eventually leading to two failed suicide attempts.

Then things changed. I remember lying in a hospital bed after getting my stomach pumped, the taste of liquid charcoal still on my lips. The doctors and nurses kept asking why I tried to end my life. I didn't have a suitable answer. Or at least, I felt my answers weren't good enough.

But I eventually came up with an answer. I didn't really want to die so much as I wanted to stop the unbearable emotional pain that I had struggled with my whole life. This feeling of being a born loser (as a kid, I felt a kinship to Charlie Brown). Of worthlessness. Of never being good enough at anything. Of hopelessness.

The first change I made was to stop drinking and start going to Alcoholics Anonymous. Not saying it's the right answer for every alcoholic. But it helped me. I attended other 12-step groups, such as Al-Anon, Codependents Anonymous, and Adult Children of Alcoholics. I joined an informal women's support group. Eventually, I separated from and divorced my abusive husband.

Most important of all, I began a journey of self-discovery, healing, and exploration. I read tons of self-help books. Some were helpful, others not so much. I explored a range of spiritual and religious paths, including Wicca, A Course in Miracles, and Buddhism.

After a few years, I could honestly say I loved myself. I was a good person. A caring person. A creative person. I still had a few demons, areas of my life in which self-doubt stemming from trauma liked to creep in. I still do today after twenty-five years of sobriety.

I still have to deal with anxiety and PTSD from time to time. But it no longer holds me prisoner the way it once did. It doesn't affect my professional life as a writer the way it used to. I can read my previously published books and truly enjoy them. I don't think they're all that and a bag of chips. But I enjoy reading them and appreciate why other people do too.

I first started writing when I was a teenager, typing out stories on an old manual Smith Corona typewriter. My first story was a blatant rip-off of H. G. Wells's *The Time Machine*. I dreamed of one day becoming a professional novelist.

Every month, I read *Writer's Digest* magazine from cover to cover, becoming a devotee of Lawrence Block's fiction column. I scoured *Writer's Market* for places where I could submit my stories. Along the way, I accumulated a nice stack of rejection letters.

In high school, I added acoustic guitar to my creative outlets. I had a natural talent and often played for friends and family. In college, I majored in journalism, while also taking creative writing and music courses. And then creative self-doubt crept in.

I sought gigs to make a little money playing guitar but didn't know how to play electric. The public's interest in folk rock was fading, replaced by the power rock ballads of the '80s. I felt out of my depth. What few gigs I secured made me feel like an imposter.

When I applied for journalism internships, I was rejected by all that I applied for. When I searched for a job post-graduation, all I could find was a minimum-wage position at a tiny rural radio station that made the fictional WKRP look like a corporate behemoth. My official title was "news director," but I was the entire news staff. My duties comprised doing little more than rewriting stories in the local paper and working as the morning drive DJ.

Eventually, I shoved both the writing and the music aside. I got a horrendous job at a big corporation. When I came out as transgender, they fired me. For the next few years, I did what I had to in order to survive. Not all of it legal. I never had a career, just a long series of low-level jobs. What a failure I was.

Not until I was in my mid-forties did I once again take up writing. A friend invited me to take part in National Novel Writing Month. If you're not familiar with it, it's a personal challenge event with thousands of participants all over the world. The goal is to write a fifty-thousand-word novel during the month of November.

It seemed like such a daunting challenge. I'd only written short stories when I was a teen. And here I was, not having written a story of any length for thirty years. Could I write a fifty-thousand-word novel in a month? Turned out I could. I hit my goal shortly after Thanksgiving in 2007. I still have the T-shirt.

That event relaunched my passion for writing career. For several years, I wrote stories and took part in local critique groups while learning the craft. I discovered there were many skills to master, including story structure, scene structure, dialogue, narration, and character development.

I reached the point of entertaining the idea of being published. I had grown up believing that going through a traditional publisher was the only "legitimate" path to publication. So I began searching for a literary agent to represent me. I sent queries, synopses, and partial manuscripts to ninety literary agents before one agreed to represent me. While that may not be an uncommon statistic, it was a lot of rejection to deal with. A whole lotta "no thank yous."

Eventually, one of the Big Five publishers bought my

first two novels. I believed my ship had come in. But no. The publisher did little to promote the book, and they ended the series after two books. I wondered if I'd ever be a "real" author with a career.

But I refused to give up. They say that failure isn't getting knocked down but not getting back up when you do. So, despite the blows to my ego from the poor sales and series cancellation, I pressed ahead. I came up with a new series. But this time, I chose to become my own publisher. I hired a team of editors, cover designers, et al. I've been indie ever since.

I have struggled with imposter syndrome. Harsh reviews have sent me questioning whether I had what it took to be a "real" writer. Was I smart enough, talented enough, and educated enough to write stories that readers would love?

Then I learned to use the tools I gained in my recovery from alcoholism and from Buddhism and my support groups. These tools helped me dismantle the negativity that ensnares so many creative people.

I now enjoy writing, even when it gets hard. I enjoy creating interesting characters and telling compelling stories. I even enjoy editing those stories, fixing plot holes, and cutting down info dumps. I enjoy sharing my work with the world. I can read back through my previously published works and feel a sense of pride for what I've created. I don't feel the need to compare myself or my work to that of other authors. I don't view my books as less-than.

Maybe one day I will make a living from my writing. Maybe I'll eventually be nominated and win an award. Maybe one day the *New York Times* will review one of my books. Or maybe not. Either way, I've learned to trust the process and savor the journey every step along the way.

I am proud to be part of an amazing community of

writers. We are such fascinating people with stories to tell. Each of us has our own unique author journey.

But so many of us suffer from creative self-doubt despite writing remarkable stories and despite so many of us winning awards, accolades, and financial success. That insidious voice of self-doubt creeps in to sabotage our enjoyment of the process and the appreciation of our work.

This doesn't have to be the case.

You can reclaim enjoyment of writing. You can once again feel a sense of pride toward your finished stories, whether they've been published or not. You deserve to be free of the fear of being "found out" as an imposter.

So, I am sharing what I've learned about overcoming self-doubt and feelings of worthlessness. I'm offering you the tools that work for me to face down those voices that tell us we are imposters in danger of being found out. I'm showing you a way through or around the blocks that come up to impede your journey.

I am not a therapist or licensed counselor, but I know what it feels like to struggle with these negative thoughts daily. I found a way through and will show you that way.

I can't guarantee miracles. I can only show you what worked for me. It took me years to work through my insecurities. And I still struggle with fears, mostly financial. The voices of depression, anxiety, and trauma still call my name. But by using the tools I've acquired over the past twenty-five years, I keep them at bay.

Beyond these tools, I address several aspects of the author's journey that can be a minefield of negativity then show you how to navigate your way through them.

Some of what I share might seem a bit woo-woo. That's okay. I'll try to keep the woo to a minimum, but sometimes, new ideas can feel foreign or ridiculous or a waste of time. I used to think that gratitude lists were as corny as Cobb County, Georgia (apologies to residents of Cobb County).

But they turned out to be remarkably effective in combating negativity. So try to keep an open mind.

This book is no substitute for professional help. As I've said before, I am not a counselor, therapist, psychologist, or psychiatrist. I hold no advanced degrees. My recovery program included seeing a therapist and even going on antidepressants for a time. They helped me.

If you are struggling with depression (especially suicidal depression), bipolar disorder, PTSD, or some other severe mental disorder, it may be a good idea to get professional help, if you can. This is your journey. Assess your needs as best you can and get the help you require.

One last point. Give yourself time. Time to familiarize yourself with the tools and ideas I share. Time to undo the damage from years or decades of trauma and other negativity. Time to heal. Time to grow. These are tools, not a cure. Take what you like and leave the rest.

I wish you all the best in your creative journey.

1

What Is Creative Self-Doubt?

Before we start exploring the solutions, we must understand the problem that we are dealing with. Imposter syndrome and writer's block may seem like different issues, but they are different expressions of the same issue: creative self-doubt.

What is creative self-doubt? At its most basic, creativity is fear. Fear of the uncertainty that is inherent in creativity. Fear of failure. Fear of success. Fear of acting without permission. Fear of change. Fear of staying the same. Fear of getting stuck. Fear of moving ahead into parts unknown.

Creative self-doubt is that voice in our brain that tells us that our creative works are crap, that we have no talent, or that we are a fraud in danger of being found out and punished. It tells us not to bother trying, because whatever we put on the page will be embarrassingly awful and unfixable.

Even if we knocked it out of the park with a previous project, this voice of doom insists that success was a fluke. We don't have any more good ideas. We don't have real talent. We don't have the proper education or training to make it as a creative.

Creative self-doubt tells us that no matter how much success we may experience, no matter how many awards or glowing reviews we may receive, our creative works are disappointingly subpar. And when the rest of the world realizes how awful our work really is, there will be hell to pay. They will rip us to shreds, stripping us of any awards and the right to call ourselves authors, much less bestsellers. No one will ever buy our work again. We might as well quit now.

Sound familiar? If so, you're not alone. And you're in the right place.

Creative people across all forms of media struggle with this nagging voice that persists in telling us we're not good enough. We don't have what it takes.

Even super-successful artists and writers have struggled with this. Whether you call it imposter syndrome or comparisonitis or writer's block or simply insecurity, it's ubiquitous in the creative world. There's always someone better, and by comparison, our work feels like a pathetic joke.

We struggle with weaponized terms like "real author" or "real artist." Who gets to decide what "real" is?

In the movie *The Matrix*, Morpheus asks Neo, "What is real? How do you define 'real'? If you're talking about what you can feel, what you can smell, what you can taste and see, then 'real' is simply electrical signals interpreted by your brain."

In the context of our creative work, "real" doesn't have any substantive meaning. It's nothing more than gaslighting, a delusion.

If you write, you are a writer. If you have finished a story, whether or not it's been published, you are an author. Period. "Real" is merely a weapon our insecurity uses against us to keep us from creating and trying new things.

WHAT IS CREATIVE SELF-DOUBT?

Why do we have this self-doubt? Where does it come from? Some of us received unduly harsh criticism from a teacher or mentor who should have encouraged us. Maybe some of us were born this way. I've struggled with insecurity as far back as I can remember.

Part of what makes self-doubt so pervasive is the uncertainty. Every time we write a story, we are creating something new. We're not making widgets, each one the same as the last. With every story, we are creating new characters, new adventures, and new worlds. Even within a series, we are taking our existing characters and pushing them further than we have before. We are presenting them and thus ourselves with new challenges.

With each new story, we are taking a chance that our words may not resonate the way we would like. Even if our last story garnered glowing reviews, there is no guarantee the next one will. We are always treading new ground and facing new risks. With so much on the line, so many unknowns, self-doubt is inevitable.

But self-doubt doesn't have to control us or rob us of the joy of creation. We can retrain that part of our minds to work with us rather than against us. We can grow so that when we look back on our work, we can treasure it for what it is without embarrassment. We can go through our rough drafts or early efforts without stabbing our souls with hateful thoughts. We can carve doors in the seemingly impenetrable creative block and find a way through.

We can even explore new avenues in our chosen craft, or look into learning new crafts without the unbearable sense of doom and hopelessness. If you're a writer, maybe you will experiment with other genres. If you're an artist, perhaps you will try out new media.

The blank page or canvas or block of stone or new role will no longer seem the threatening cave of impossibilities or overwhelm you.

But I want to make one thing very clear. This isn't a simple fix. There is no affirmation or meditation that will make your creative self-doubt vanish overnight. Rather, we are unlearning years of negativity. We are shaving away at its power one micro-thin layer at a time. Give the tools time to work.

As I mentioned in the introduction, I struggled with self-doubt since early childhood. The voices of negativity have not completely vanished from my mind. But they no longer hold sway as they once did. Discovering a flaw in a story doesn't feel like a stake to the heart, sending me spiraling down a well of worthlessness. It's simply something that needs to be fixed.

This is a journey of recovery. It is a quest to rediscover our joy in our chosen craft. It is an adventure to slay our own dragons, or at the very least train them to follow our commands.

Are you ready to join me?

Let's start with the different voices inside your head. I'm not talking about the voices of your characters but rather the different voices that show up when it's time to work on your writing.

First, there is the creative voice, what some call their muse. That voice is you. It has been with you since childhood. It was what inspired you to write. The creative voice likes to play "What if?" It likes to imagine new characters, worlds, stories, and plot twists.

What if there was a bounty hunter who was transgender and who enjoyed cosplaying as Wonder Woman? What if there was an international spy that suddenly developed OCD after being tortured by the enemy? What if there was a tattoo artist who discovered a bag full of money next to her boyfriend's dead body? What if a man develops a crush on a woman he met at the supermarket, but he assumes she's dating someone because he misheard a phone conversation?

WHAT IS CREATIVE SELF-DOUBT?

Our creative voice doesn't worry about info dumps or spelling or comma splices or POV shifts or plot holes. This voice is in love with the thrill of inventing stories and putting them on paper. This is the voice that's in charge when we're creating a story outline and our rough draft. This voice is playful and loves to experiment.

Next comes our editorial voice or inner editor. This aspect of our mind supports our creative voice. Our editorial voice doesn't seek to tear apart what the creative voice has created. It takes what the creative voice has laid down and makes it better. The editorial voice is a mensch, a fixer, a polisher.

This inner editor sees an info dump and asks, "What details in this info dump do I need to keep, and what is pulling the reader out of the story?"

When the editor recognizes awkward dialogue, it asks, "How can I reword this so that the language flows more naturally and keeps the reader engaged?" There's no shaming. No humiliation. The editorial voice is simply seeking to improve what's already there.

The creative voice and the editorial voice are on the same team. Their goal is the same—to tell the best story you can. Because they are both you. *You* want to tell the best story you can.

Sometimes the editorial voice jumps in too soon, such as when the creative voice is writing the rough draft or the outline. When this happens, it can gum up the works. We can get so focused on proper structure, grammar, spelling, and factual details that our creative voice gets overwhelmed. Our muse packs up her bat and ball and goes home.

When this happens, we have to remind our editorial voice to wait their turn. First, we create, *then* we fix. Whatever mistakes we make in our rough draft we can rectify later.

And when you revise, don't leave your muse locked

in the closet, bound and gagged. Let her out because sometimes, she comes up with better ideas than she did the first go-round. Not only can this help you tell a better story, but it can make the revision process a little more playful and fun. Let your muse and editor work together when the time is right.

Besides the muse and the editor, there is often an all-too-familiar third voice—the shaming voice. I like to call it the troll. The troll isn't a team player. It doesn't get along with either the muse or the editor. It isn't seeking to improve your story. The troll wants to crap on everything you've worked so hard on, or better yet, to keep you from writing anything in the first place.

The troll or shaming voice likes to pretend it's your editorial voice. But its goal isn't to make your work better. It just wants to stifle creativity and leave you feeling badly about yourself as an author and about everything you've written.

Where the editorial voice might ask, "How can I make this scene more engaging?" the troll just states, "This is crap. It's boring. The characters are milquetoast. The world isn't believable. No one will want to read this."

Like the creative voice and the editorial voice, the shaming voice is a part of us. It's not a bad part of us. It's where we are wounded. It's where we are afraid to fail or even afraid to succeed. It is the embodiment of our creative self-doubt. And if we want to grow on our author journey, we will need to learn how to handle the little troll inside of us so that it doesn't control either our creative or editorial process.

By freeing ourselves from this negative, shaming voice, we can not only write better stories but appreciate all the work we put into them. We can reread them years later and be proud of our efforts. We will no longer feel the need to cringe when someone compliments our work. We will

WHAT IS CREATIVE SELF-DOUBT?

no longer feel like an imposter when our work receives the recognition it deserves. We can enjoy and celebrate all aspects of our writing journey.

That is the goal of this book. I am providing you with basic tools that will help you take back control of your creative process and free yourself from the troll's shaming and fearmongering. I will also explore scenarios in which creative self-doubt can arise in your author journey and how to work through these situations.

Welcome to your breakthrough.

2

We All Feel Like Imposters

Most authors struggle with creative self-doubt at some point in their career. But this isn't an issue faced only by authors. Other creatives do as well, including many celebrities.

Do a web search for celebrities who've had imposter syndrome, and you will come up with quite a few: Tom Hanks, Tina Fey, Maisie Williams, Awkwafina, Meryl Streep, Ryan Reynolds. The list is endless.

These are people who have proven repeatedly they have the goods. And yet they each have that inner troll telling them the opposite.

Many of the artists and actors and authors who have struggled with substance abuse and even taken their own lives were dealing with this same issue. Imposter syndrome can be a big part of clinical depression, this feeling that we are worthless, that whatever praise we get is out of pity rather than a recognition of the quality of our work.

Just the other day, Stephen Colbert stated on his show that he continued to suffer from imposter syndrome even after over twenty-five years of being a comedy writer and performer for shows like *The Daily Show*, *Saturday Night*

Live, *The Colbert Report*, and *Late Night with Stephen Colbert*. He has won nearly two dozen awards, including Emmys and Grammys. And yet every day when he has to put together a new show, he feels like a fraud.

In a 2013 interview with *Rookie* magazine, Emma Watson, who shined as Hermione Granger in the *Harry Potter* movies, said, "It's almost like the better I do, the more my feeling of inadequacy actually increases, because I'm just going, 'Any moment, someone's going to find out I'm a total fraud, and that I don't deserve any of what I've achieved.'"

In her HBO concert documentary *Lady Gaga Presents the Monster Ball Tour: At Madison Square Garden*, Lady Gaga explained, "I still sometimes feel like a loser kid in high school, and I just have to pick myself up and tell myself that I'm a superstar every morning so that I can get through this day and be for my fans what they need for me to be."

If you're familiar with Gaga's work, you'll see this theme run through many of her songs.

After Jodie Foster won her first Oscar, she was convinced that someone would find out that she was "a fraud" and the Academy would come knocking on her door demanding the statue back, insisting they'd made a mistake.

Lupita Nyong'o explained that winning an Oscar made her imposter syndrome worse because the expectations and pressure on her were so much higher. She feared she wouldn't live up to those expectations.

No quantity of success or accolades will ever be enough to drive out that troll of self-doubt. We can't shove awards in its face and say, "See, I'm not a fraud."

The troll only laughs at us and tells us, "Wow, there will be hell to pay when everyone finds out how untalented you really are."

Soon, we fear our success as much as, if not more than, failure.

But there is hope. The troll doesn't get to have the final say.

We can't hide from that shaming, fear-mongering voice, but we can take away its power to terrorize us. To do that, we must go deep. We must face this part of ourselves and use the tools I share to disarm the troll and reclaim our joy and love of writing.

The process will not be easy or quick. This isn't a quick-fix kind of problem. As we say in Alcoholics Anonymous, we didn't get sick overnight. We will not get better overnight.

This is a gradual process of healing. It's a process of acknowledging and letting go. It's a path of gentleness and willingness. We can't force it or rush it. But if we are persistent, we will see astounding results.

Right now, you may not see how talented you are. You can't recognize how entertaining your work is or how amazing your future writing will be. But together, we can clear away the delusions, free ourselves of the negativity, and open the way for a more joyful journey as authors.

If you haven't already done so, I strongly encourage you to develop friendships with other authors, especially other authors who are roughly at the same level you are and who may write in the same genre as you. There are a lot of groups online and in person for this very purpose.

When I was starting out, I found a lot of local critique groups via Meetup.com. There are also professional groups that focus on specific genres or who have the same approach to writing or publishing as you. Seek them out.

I'm currently a member of Sisters in Crime, Mystery Writers of America, Queer Crime Writers, and the Alliance of Independent Authors. Some require a paid membership, but most aren't expensive. Find the support organizations that fit your writing.

Connecting with other writers is a great way to stay abreast of the ever-changing publishing industry. But more importantly, these friendships help us feel less isolated as writers. You'll discover you aren't alone in feeling like an imposter. And in doing so, you'll see cracks in the troll's threats of doom.

If we're all imposters, then who's a "real" writer, anyway? None of us. And all of us. We're all just creating stories, borrowing and reinventing ideas, and playing "what if."

The awards don't make us any more or less "real." Neither does any other marker of success.

They might help us pay the light bill. They might help us reach more readers. But if we let go of this idea that they are indicators of talent or worth, then they have less power to rob us of our joy of creation, whether or not we achieve them.

If you're writing stories that are meaningful to you, then you are not an imposter. You are a storyteller. You are a writer. You are an author.

3

Using Meditation to Release Self-Doubt

It's time to get to the good stuff—the tools that will help you dethrone your troll of insecurity. The first tool is meditation.

Okay, I see you've got all kinds of red flags going up. You may wonder what meditation has to do with writing.

Or more likely, you're thinking that you can't do meditation. That meditation isn't your thing. It's too woo-woo. Your mind is too busy. Maybe you have ADHD. You can't sit in a lotus position. You aren't interested in becoming a Zen master. What will I suggest next? A juice cleanse?

Don't worry. No juice cleanses. We have livers and kidneys to handle that job. No one is trying to turn you into a Zen Buddhist. You don't need to break out the incense or candles or massage spa music. We're not casting a spell or anything. This isn't magic.

Also, I can't sit in a lotus position either. I'm a middle-aged woman with bad knees. If I forced myself into a lotus position, I would require a crowbar and a team of physical therapists to help me walk again.

Set aside all that emotional baggage and hear me out.

Meditation is a powerful tool for taking back your authorial career. And you can do it. I will show you.

Meditation isn't some mysterious woo-woo thing. There are many kinds of meditation. But essentially, they all are ways to help us focus and let go of negativity.

We're going to use meditation to quiet the chatter in our minds and disarm the troll that is plaguing our experience as a writer and robbing us of the joy we deserve from it.

When I meditate, I sit normally on a couch or chair. See? It's pretty simple. No joint-twisting position. No special clothing. Nothing to worry about.

Oh, and that busy-busy mind? Don't worry about that either. We all have that. It won't be a problem. I promise. If you have to tap your finger or play with a fidget spinner while you do it, by all means, go for it.

It is important that you understand that meditation is a practice, not a performance. No one will be judging you. No one-star reviews.

The more you do it, the more you will get out of it. Notice I didn't say the better you will be at it. There is no better or worse. It is simply a practice. It is the doing that matters.

So, why meditate? It helps us uncouple our minds from the rantings of our inner critic. It can also change the recordings playing in the back of our mind, replacing the negative with positive.

Meditation isn't magic. It's a gradual healing and reprogramming of the mind. It is intentional rather than reactive. That is important to understand. We are taking the wheel, making conscious choices in how we respond

USING MEDITATION TO RELEASE SELF-DOUBT 15

both physically and emotionally to every situation in our author journey.

At the same time, meditation is gentle rather than forceful. It's motivated by love rather than shame.

Even if you struggle with depression and low self-esteem like I have, there is love inside of you. You wouldn't have picked up this book otherwise. There is some core part of you that knows you deserve to be loved, or at least desperately wants to be loved.

We're going to connect you to that love. If you can't find that love inside you, then borrow some from me. I love you. I don't know you, but I already love you. And we're going to let that love guide us. Okay? It's going to be all right.

So here we go. Find a comfortable place. Preferably a quiet place. A place that you can close your eyes for just a few minutes. It can be a couch or a chair or the floor or on a bus or even the toilet. There have been times when I've had to meditate in the restroom stall at work to deal with anxiety or stress. Do what ya gotta do, right? Work with what you've got. Do the best you can. It will be good enough.

I like to listen to relaxing music when I meditate. Something soothing without words, using an app on my phone or laptop. Some people prefer to listen to classical music, nature sounds, or even silence. Whatever you prefer is fine. Don't make it a big thing. Keep it simple.

We're seeking to relax and focus our minds as best we can. If someone starts running a leaf blower outside, that's okay. We'll work with what we've got.

You can meditate with eyes shut or open. Do whatever works for you. You set the rules here. You decide your process. I'm simply here sharing what I do.

If you want to light a candle or some incense, by all means, do. Be sure to put it out when you're done. I once forgot I left a candle burning and… never mind. Another story for another time.

Now that you're in your meditation spot with whatever audio environment you have, take in a deep breath through your nose. Feel your chest expand as air fills your lungs. Feels good, doesn't it?

Now exhale through your mouth. Blow it all out. Relax your chest.

Do it all over again. Inhale, filling your body with oxygen. And exhale, releasing carbon dioxide. Again, breathe in, breathe out. Simple.

Focus your mind on the physical sensation of air coming in and air going out. Just that. In. Out. In. Out. In. Out. Chest expanding. Chest relaxing. Expanding. Relaxing.

Your mind will wander. Hoo boy, will it wander. One second, you're focusing on your breath. Next thing you know, your mind is barreling down some rabbit hole of thought. Focusing on that scene you just wrote. Or this month's sales. Or next month's launch. Or some drama going on at your day job. Or your kids or your spouse or the dog vomiting on the carpet or the leaf blowers droning outside.

Whatever it is, whenever you find your mind wandering, gently bring it back to the meditation. To the now. No shame. No negativity. Just refocus on the breath. In. Out. Expanding. Relaxing.

When your mind wanders again, which it will do repeatedly, keep gently bringing it back to the breath. The wandering is part of the process. So no shame, okay?

Try it for a minute. Set a timer if you like. Just breathing in, breathing out, focusing on the physical sensation. Gently refocusing whenever your mind wanders.

If that works, try it for five or fifteen minutes.

Not so bad, is it? All we're doing is connecting our mind with our body in this present moment. If you have an itch, it's okay to scratch it. If you feel a tightness or tension somewhere, acknowledge it and imagine letting it go as you exhale. We're just connecting our mind and our body with now. Gentle, gentle, gentle. Release, relax.

If you fall asleep, that's okay. You probably needed the rest. No worries.

You could work your way up to thirty minutes or an hour if you wanted to, but let's take it slow at first. Remember, gentle. Keep it easy. Don't complicate it. We're making gradual changes here. There is no recipe for instant enlightenment.

Our goal right now is to get out of our heads and connect with our bodies. We are distancing ourselves from our inner critic, even if it's just for a moment or a few seconds at a time.

For a lot of us, this is an unfamiliar experience. Our troll doesn't want to let go. It will try to convince us that this doesn't work, that meditation is a waste of time, that you are a hopeless failure of a writer, and that whatever you've written isn't even worthy to wrap fish in. But the troll is a liar.

When you feel you're ready for the next step, let's add a little something to it. When you inhale, imagine you are inhaling positive energy. Love, joy, abundance, serenity, creativity, whatever word or idea works for you. It can be love from your friends and family, love from God or your Higher Power or the Universe or me. As you breathe in, feel that positive energy fill your body.

Now imagine all of that positivity you're breathing in is wrapping itself around your tension and anxiety and self-doubt and negativity, like oxygen molecules bonding to carbon molecules to form carbon dioxide. Now blow it all out and release it.

It's as if we are taking out the trash, using our breath to fill us with positivity and release the negativity. All we're doing is gathering it up and getting rid of it. We're taking out the trash. We don't hate the negativity. We simply don't need it anymore.

Feel your entire body relax as you let it all go. Inhale positivity. Exhale negativity. Over and over again.

This is a gradual process. You probably won't notice a change right away. Not in a single breathing cycle. Or even in a single meditation session. That's okay. This a practice, not a performance. We are not striving for perfection.

When we meditate on a regular basis, as we focus on opening ourselves up to positivity and letting go of negativity, our perspective will gradually improve. We are being intentional. We are being gentle. We are being loving.

A similar approach is to imagine you are sitting with a bunch of your fellow writers, people who are roughly at the same level as you professionally. If you are a beginner still learning the basics, then think of people you've connected to in person or online who are learning right along with you. If you have several books under your belt, imagine your fellow published authors, especially those in your same genre.

These people may be in a local critique group with you or authors you've met at a conference or who you've connected with via social media. Just imagine you are sitting in a room with them.

Think about how much you respect them and their writing. Now, with every exhalation, send them love. Imagine tendrils of loving energy flowing from you and into them every time you exhale. Keep sending it. Feels good to send them love, doesn't it?

Guess what? A lot of these authors you're sending love also respect you and your work. Doesn't matter if your inner critic doesn't believe it right now or doesn't think you deserve it. They do. Deal with it.

With every inhalation, imagine them sending tendrils of love and respect to you. Don't fight it. Just let it in. Feels

USING MEDITATION TO RELEASE SELF-DOUBT

good to let it in. Let it flow through you. Let it fill you, just as the oxygen fills your lungs. Allow it to energize you.

Breathe in love from your peers. Breathe out love for them. Back and forth, the energy flows. It doesn't matter whether you believe this energy is real. What is real are the pathways you are creating in your brain.

We are writing new code. That code says, "I am loved. I'm not going to fight it. I'm going to let that love in. My work is respected. I will not dismiss that respect. I will not fight it or dispute it. I'm going to accept and embrace it."

Breathe in love. Breathe out love. In. Out. Love. Love. Respect. Respect.

Not so scary, is it? We're just connecting to our bodies. Connecting to our minds. Connecting to our peers. Connecting to our work. We are creating new thought patterns about ourselves and our writing. We are literally reprogramming our brain one neural pathway at a time. Going over it and over it until the pathways of love and joy and respect are stronger than the old pathways of self-doubt, fear, and shame.

4

Affirmations

Now that you're getting a feel for how to use meditation to free yourself from the grip of creative self-doubt, let's add another tool to your toolbox: affirmations.

Affirmations, or mantras, as some people call them, are positive, intentional statements designed to reprogram our brain, to change which thoughts resonate with us and which do not.

Just as the best way to get an earworm out of your head is with a different song, the best way to remove the negative thought patterns is with positive thought patterns.

You can say them aloud or just in your head, depending on your comfort level. Saying them aloud can give them a little more power. You can do a session of a single minute or up to fifteen minutes. In one session, you repeat a single affirmation or several, one after another.

Give yourself time to consider the meaning of each affirmation, ten or fifteen seconds at least. Not just its literal meaning but what it means to you. Look at each word individually and the affirmation as a whole.

Pay attention to the emotions that arise with each

affirmation. Imagine what your author journey looks like if these affirmations are true. Because they are probably truer than you realize.

I have found a great app to help with this. The I Am app, which is free for both iOS and Android phones, provides affirmation notifications throughout the day. You can do a dedicated affirmation session for one minute, five minutes, or fifteen minutes, in which the app cycles through a series of affirmations based on a topic you choose.

The I Am app also encourages you to add your own affirmations, which can be helpful when we are trying to change our thoughts and feelings about our writing. You can create affirmations that target where you are in your author journey and with your creative self-doubt, as well as where you want to be.

There are plenty of other resources, such as books and podcasts. Or you can simply write your own affirmations on index cards or in a Word document and recite them that way. Use whatever tools fit your lifestyle. There is no right or wrong.

Here are some affirmations I've come up with for myself:

I love writing.
I enjoy editing and making my stories more entertaining.
I'm grateful for the people who enjoy my writing.
My writing attracts readers who buy my books.
I am a talented author.
I am proud of the stories that I've written and published.

You can write your own affirmations based on whatever specific needs you struggle with.

If you feel like an imposter, focus on affirming that you are a talented author who writes entertaining stories that readers enjoy.

If you struggle with the idea of being a "real" author, affirm that you are.

If you struggle with aspects of writing, revising, or any other part of the story creation process, focus on those elements with positive thoughts.

You don't have to concentrate solely on writing-related affirmations either. You can do affirmations on general self-esteem, health, self-image, relationships, money, marketing, entrepreneurship, or whatever. A holistic approach that touches on a variety of issues you are struggling with can be helpful.

You can also include affirmations for things that you already believe and accept about yourself. Sometimes, mixing these in with more aspirational affirmations can help you overcome those feelings of resistance that may arise.

For example, if you enjoy writing but stress out during the revision process, you can have affirmations that cover all the bases.

I am great at creating new characters and stories.
I enjoy improving my rough drafts.
I love the drafting process.
I love the problem-solving aspect of editing.
I enjoy discovering what happens next in my stories.
The characters I create are complex and nuanced.
I have a good sense of story structure.
I am confident in my ability to polish my work.

The momentum you get from affirmations you already know are true can help you power through the resistance you may feel when you hit affirmations that you are less certain of.

The resistance is normal. When you hit an affirmation that flies in the face of your creative self-doubt, that little troll inside you will shout, "Fake news! Not true!" That's okay. If you didn't have any resistance, you wouldn't need to do affirmations.

The goal here is to rewrite the pathways in the brain. This isn't a one-and-done process. You will have to go over the same ground repeatedly to see some results. It may feel like a "you said, the troll said" situation for a while.

"I am a talented author," you affirm.

"No, you're not," your inner troll replies.

"I craft *interesting*, engaging characters."

And the troll predictably responds, "Nuh-uh."

"People enjoy my stories."

"Not everyone!"

You get the idea. It can go back and forth. But you know what? The more you repeat these positive affirmations, the more they will take hold. You will start to believe them. And they will improve the trajectory of your author journey.

5

Willing to See Things Differently

Sometimes it feels as if our inner troll has the last word, that our negative thoughts have calcified into a wall of stone blocking our path. We look at our work and immediately, unconsciously go negative. It's a gag reflex, our default setting. We simply cannot imagine any other way of honestly assessing what we've created. We may view ourselves the same way, as worthless, talentless, hopeless imposters.

There is a way through this wall of stone. There is a door, and we have the key to unlock it. That key is willingness.

That door was always there. But negativity has a way of narrowing our perspective and hiding it from view. All we see is the stone wall. It blocks out potential solutions preemptively before we even realize them.

The thought that maybe our creative works have worth? Our negativity doesn't even want us to entertain that idea. It firmly says, "No! Don't look there. That's arrogant. How dare you think of yourself as anything but a hack!"

But willingness can change that. Willingness opens our perspective. It shows us the door and unlocks it. It dares shamelessly to entertain new possibilities and perspectives.

Maybe, just maybe, our extreme negative thinking toward ourselves and our work isn't as honest an assessment as the little troll would have us believe.

Maybe we do have some talent and skill. Maybe comparing ourselves to other authors on different paths with different experiences and different access isn't fair or honest. Maybe it's okay to look for the good in our work and in ourselves. Maybe it's okay to appreciate some of the creative choices we've made. Maybe.

Willingness isn't magic. All it's doing is turning "nope" into "maybe." Willingness allows us to question our assumptions. Because maybe our assumptions are built on flawed logic and bad data. We can be willing to see things differently and, by doing so, get a more complete view of our situation.

When I use the I Am app on my phone, sometimes an affirmation come up that triggers resistance in me. Not just a little resistance but a *lot* of resistance.

Something like "I am a successful businessperson" may trigger my troll to say, "No you aren't." And that negative response contains a grain of truth. I'm not earning a profit, much less a living, as an author. So I can't be much of a success, now, can I?

When one of these affirmations comes up, I insert the words "willing to." So I could say, "I am willing to seeing myself as a successful businessperson." Or even, "I am willing to see where I have been successful."

Because while I may not yet be earning a profit with my writing, I can see aspects of my author business in which I have been successful. I am usually successful at live events where I sell and sign books. I know how to attract readers who enjoy what I write. I know how to engage with them. And when I do, at least half the time, they buy a book. That's pretty successful.

What I am doing is planting seeds of doubt in my

negativity. I'm countering my self-doubt with doubt. Fighting fire with fire.

My negativity says, "You're a failure. You've been publishing books for five years and are still in the red."

To which I respond, "I am willing to see the areas where I am successful and capitalize on them. I am willing to explore alternative approaches. I am willing to learn how to generate more income. I am willing to believe that success is still an option."

I do not know how I'm going to turn this around and make my author business a success. I don't have any definite answers. But I am willing and open to change. I am willing to see things differently.

We may not know how to see things differently. We may be totally unaware of where and how we are getting things right. We may be totally blind to the good qualities in our work. Our troll wants us convinced that our current negative perspective is the true one. It's not interested in deluding ourselves with woo-woo thinking (or so the troll tells us).

But what if the troll is the delusional one? What if it's dead wrong in its assessment of our work? What if there are factors that we don't know that we don't know? Issues and perspectives that we haven't even considered? We can use doubt as a tool to turn things around.

Our negativity may tell us that we don't have what it takes to be a "real author." But let's get real about this "real" nonsense.

A writer is someone who writes, be it novels, short stories, poetry, memoirs, etc. An author is a writer who has created a literary work, whether or not it's been published, no matter how good or bad it may be.

If you do the work, then you are a writer. If you complete a work, you are an author. You either are or you aren't. "Real" is a meaningless qualifier that our troll uses to attack our credibility.

So back to willingness. Let's get active here and take a major step. We're going to do some affirmations. Don't panic. We are simply sitting down wherever we are and focusing our minds on a few major affirmations. You can do it at your kitchen table, in the restroom at work, or on a noisy, bouncy bus. Just focus your mind as best you can. Okay? Okay.

Let's start with a simple affirmation.

I am willing to see things differently.

Just repeat it over and over in your mind for a minute. Consider each word and what it means.

"I am willing..." We're unlocking the door. We're entertaining new possibilities.

"...to see things..." We're focusing on our perspective, our assumptions, and our habitual thought processes. We're opening it all up on how we see everything, especially as it relates to our creative work.

"...differently." Ooh, this implies change. Scary! It's the unknown, because we're not really sure how we should see things. But that's okay. We are opening up to new possibilities. We aren't committing ourselves to anything, necessarily. We are simply widening our gaze and taking inventory of what we may not have yet considered.

Keep repeating the affirmation and consider what it means to you. What are some things you could see differently? How might you see them differently? What are some of your previous assumptions that are worth revisiting?

Once you've done that for a few minutes, let's get a little more specific. Try this next affirmation.

I am willing to see myself differently.

Hoo boy! That opens a whole can of worms. Seeing ourselves differently? Yikes. But maybe we've had blinders on. We don't necessarily have to come to any conclusions.

But at least we can be open to new ways of seeing ourselves, our goals, our joys, our self-talk, our insecurities, and our accomplishments. We're opening our eyes and looking deeply and unflinchingly.

Just repeat the affirmation slowly aloud or silently for a few minutes and consider what it might mean for you.

Once you've done that and you're ready for more, let's try another one. You don't have to do this all in one sitting. You can do one affirmation today and the next affirmation tomorrow or next week. Affirmations are flexible.

Here's the next affirmation:

I am willing to see my writing differently.

This is a bold step. We're open to new ways of seeing what we've written. That includes rough drafts, abandoned projects, published works, all of it. We are willing to see them all with fresh eyes.

Repeat the affirmation over and over. *I am willing to see my writing differently.*

Could we have judged our earlier work too harshly? Could we have been shaming ourselves over our rough drafts? Have we been so obsessed with the flaws in our stories that we ignored the shining gems? Have we tried to compare our early works with the polished works of more established authors in our genre? Would we be willing to entertain new perspectives on what we have created and what we are currently creating?

Okay, here are a few others to play with when you're ready.

I am willing to look at my process differently.
I am willing to look at opportunities differently.
I am willing to make different choices.

Again, all we're doing with this exercise is exploring possibilities. And really, isn't that what creativity is about? It's playing the "what if" game. What if I've been disparaging my work unnecessarily? What if people really do enjoy reading my stories? What if my writing really does connect with people in a meaningful way?

We are opening ourselves up to new ways of seeing, ways that might free us from the burdens of negativity and creative self-doubt. That is all we're doing. We are giving ourselves permission to move from blocked to open, from talking down about ourselves and our creative work to celebrating our accomplishments. We are opening ourselves up to improvement and healing. From needing to be perfect to being open to making progress.

It's okay to feel uncertain or fearful or foolish. But who knows what could happen if every day, we took one of these affirmations and canoodled it for a few minutes? No set goals. No expectations. We're just turning it over in our minds.

When I was in my twenties, my wife at the time and I took a trip to the Florida Keys and stayed in a motel on the Gulf side.

Every morning, I would sit on this old concrete dock and stare down into the water. At first, I didn't see much. Occasionally a fish swimming by. Some turtle grass waving in the current. A tiny crab scuttling along the bottom.

By the third day, I started seeing things I hadn't noticed before. Features became more familiar, and I started seeing more details. Sea anemones. Conchs. A spiny lobster living in a crevice. How had I not noticed these things before?

Sometimes we have to look at something over and over again before we really see what's there.

Have you ever misplaced something and gone looking all over for it, only to find it was in an obvious place? Because even if it was right there, staring at you, your mind had a blind spot. Something in your mind prevented you from registering it.

Something in our mind has been preventing us from seeing our true worth as an author. Maybe that something is a previous trauma. Maybe it's a lifelong insecurity. Maybe it's unreasonable expectations. Maybe it is the uncertainty that comes with creating art.

Whatever it is, we have to be willing to let it go and see things with fresh eyes. By saying that we are willing to see ourselves differently, we are giving ourselves permission to look beyond the trauma, the insecurity, the flaws, and the unreasonable expectations. Doing this helps us to see who we are and where we are. We can allow ourselves to make an honest inventory of what we bring to our writing. Not just talent but experience and education.

Life experience counts a lot. If you're in your twenties, you don't have as much life experience as compared to someone in their fifties.

Writing experience counts a lot too. The more you write, the better you will get. With each story, you try things and push your skills and internalize what works and what doesn't. What rules you can bend and how to do so effectively.

Education matters too. Not just college degrees but online webinars, reading books on writing, and taking part in critique groups and workshops. Education comes in a variety of formats.

If you are just starting out, you don't need to feel insecure about not knowing the difference between showing versus telling or accidentally switching POV characters in a scene. You will learn the rules of the craft. Just keep writing. Trust the process. Trust *your* process.

If you don't have a college education, that's okay. As I mentioned, there are many ways to learn this craft. Very few of us learn it in a formal classroom setting. I took a few creative writing classes in college, but most of what I know about storytelling came from doing the work.

Look at where you are and what you bring to the process. Be willing to grow. Where we are now does not define how far we can go.

By telling ourselves that we are willing to see our work differently, we take the scales off our eyes and allow ourselves to see more than just the flaws in our work. We can begin to see the good stuff too. We are giving ourselves permission to appreciate and enjoy what we've created, just as it is. Maybe our dialogue in a scene is a little awkward, but the character is really cool. Maybe our first page is a little info-dumpy, but some gems are hidden amongst all the fluffy narration.

Keep focusing on the willingness to change your perspective. We are changing the rules. We are disrupting our old negativity and laying the foundation for a positive, enjoyable career as an author. You have permission. Now you only need to be willing.

When you've reached the point of comfort with being willing to take the next step, when you are open to new perspectives on your work, try changing your affirmations to being ready. This is the next step toward accepting these changes in perception toward our author selves and our work.

I am ready to see my work differently.
I am ready to let go of my creative self-doubt.
I am ready to fall back in love with my writing process.
I am ready to love what I've written.
I am ready to accept my work as what it is, without shame and with whatever imperfections it may have.

Being ready is very similar to being willing. It just carries a little more confidence toward letting go of our creative self-doubt. We've entertained new possibilities, and we are prepared to take action, to challenge the little troll and its naysaying.

When you start feeling more confident in using the confirmations with no qualifiers, do so. Eventually, the training wheels have to come off. But do it in your own time at your own pace. The willingness and readiness qualifiers are simply tools to use until you don't need them anymore.

Do try to be consistent about using affirmations. Consistency is what makes them powerful. I'll fully admit I have trouble creating new habits. Doing something new every morning or whatever can be tough. My brain resists. Or my schedule changes. Or life happens. Don't fret. Do what you can, when you can, as often as you can.

6

More Tools for Your Toolbox

Meditation and affirmations aren't the only therapeutic tools you can use to free yourself from creative self-doubt. When I was early in my recovery from alcoholism, codependency, and depression, I discovered several other tools that helped me work through my trauma and related issues. Many of these same tools can free us from the grip of creative self-doubt.

When I learned about some of them, I thought they were hokey and stupid. At the time, I was not a woo-woo, touchy-feely kind of person. Don't get me wrong. I wasn't a total bitch. But I was logical and practical, a devotee of the scientific method.

I was also rebellious and suspicious of anything that reeked of mainstream. I didn't believe these therapeutic tools would help me with my self-esteem, my PTSD, or my addiction issues.

But some of the things that I thought were hokey and useless turned out to be remarkably helpful. And as a practical person, I learned not to dismiss them.

Because more than anything, I wanted to stop the deep

emotional pain I'd been living with for much of my life. I wanted to learn how to live without alcohol, codependency, and dysfunctional relationships. If these hokey tools helped me reach those goals, you bet I would use them.

In this chapter, I am simply sharing what others passed on to me. At first glance, they may not look like things that can help you with creative self-doubt. But trust a recovering alcoholic. These tools can do wonders.

This is your journey of recovery from creative self-doubt. Take what you like and leave the rest. You get to decide what works for you and what doesn't.

Gratitude Lists

The first of these tools is a gratitude list. By far, the hokiest of the hokey. When my AA sponsor told me to make a gratitude list each morning, I groaned.

"Really?" I replied to her. "A gratitude list? Every f-ing morning? What next? You gonna tell me to burn incense and sing 'Kumbaya'?"

She replied with, "Fine. Don't do it. But if you relapse and start drinking again, it's on you. I'm simply offering you the tools. It's up to you whether you use them or not."

Funny thing, she was right. Who knew?

Gratitude lists change the direction of your thinking from negative to positive. It's a subtle, gradual change, but it happens over time.

You're probably familiar with the concept of a gratitude list, but if you're not, it's a list of things you are grateful for. Each day, preferably when you first get up, you make a new list. It works best if you write it down, but creating a mental list helps too. The items on this list can be as profound or mundane as you like.

MORE TOOLS FOR YOUR TOOLBOX

Here are some of mine from when I was learning how to live without alcohol.

I am grateful to be alive today.
I am grateful to be sober.
I am grateful to have a job.
I am grateful to have food to eat.
I'm grateful to have friends who support me in my recovery.
I'm grateful to have a sponsor who is helping me stay sober.

After I finally got the nerve to leave my abusive ex-husband, I added:

I'm grateful to no longer be in an abusive relationship.
I'm grateful to be free of the crazy drama of codependency.

Additionally, we can put items on our gratitude list that are specific to our writer's journey.

I am grateful for the opportunity to write.
I'm grateful for the constructive feedback I get from critique partners.
I'm grateful for the story ideas that come to me.
I'm grateful for the lessons I'm learning on my author journey.
I'm grateful for the mistakes I make in my stories because I can learn from them as well.
I'm grateful to have finished this rough draft.
I'm grateful for this community of writers who teach me so many things and who support my efforts.
I'm grateful for the reviews I've received, including the one-star ratings.
I'm grateful for all of the mistakes that my editor found, so that I can correct them.

By composing a gratitude list each morning, we set the tone for the day. We are overriding our old habit of obsessing over what isn't working in our life by preemptively focusing on the positive things.

When we include items that address our writing, we change how we approach our writing time. We change how we view our finished works. We change how we see our writing career. Listing what we are grateful for is a gradual thing. But if we keep it up, it will yield results.

Journaling

If you've read Julia Cameron's *The Artist's Way*, you're probably already familiar with journaling, which she calls Morning Pages. If not, journaling is simply taking time each day to write down your thoughts, feelings, and experiences.

There are no hard and fast rules. If you can, journal when you first get up in the morning, perhaps right after you make your gratitude list.

If you can't, set time each day to journal. And if that doesn't fit your crazy schedule, simply journal when you can.

Some people journal on their phone or computer. Others prefer the tactile experience of putting pen to paper. But don't get hung up on finding the exact right journal or a specific pen. The benefit of journaling has nothing to do with the materials you use. The benefit comes from doing it.

Cameron suggests writing three pages each day. But you are free to write as much or as little as you see fit. The goal is to get the stuff rattling around in your head onto the paper or screen.

Maybe you've kept a journal or diary for years. Or maybe you're like me and journaling is something you occasionally try, but then you fall off the wagon after a few days. I'm not a journaler. Is that even a word? Whatever.

My point is that journaling isn't something you have to do every freakin' day. If you can, great. But if you're like me and forming that habit just doesn't take, don't despair. You can use it whenever you feel it may help.

It's a great way to get the crap out of your head. All the negativity, doubt, frustration, anger, whatever. Getting it out onto the paper or screen clears your mind so you can better focus on your creativity.

When you journal, don't worry about proper spelling or grammar or punctuation. None of that matters. Journaling is just a brain dump to clear out the clutter. Sometimes it will yield new insights into your work in progress or how to better reach your target readers or about your authorial career in general.

Don't do it for specific results. Let the results take care of themselves. Just try it for a month and see what happens.

Freewriting

Freewriting is similar to journaling, although it is more for when you get stuck in a story or feel blocked in any way.

Maybe your main character finds themselves in a no-win situation. Or you're simply not sure where to take the story next. Or you want to make a character more three-dimensional, and all you've come up with so far is a bland cardboard cutout.

When we find ourselves in this spot, we can use freewriting to brainstorm solutions. It is a way to give ourselves permission to put words on a page without worrying about grammar, spelling, plot, character, or anything. We are simply exploring ideas, allowing the bad ones to rise to the top so that we can eventually get down to where the good ones are hiding in our subconscious.

Regardless of what software you use to write—Scrivener, Microsoft Word, or anything else—I'd recommend creating a separate sheet or file for your freewriting, away from the clutter of your work in progress.

Or you may have more success changing gears completely and breaking out a pad and pen and freewriting that way. It may seem a little old-school, but the more tactile experience of writing by hand can generate enough of a mind shift that it bypasses the mental blocks your fear and uncertainty have put in your path.

With freewriting, as with journaling, don't worry about misspelled words, grammar, sentence fragments, or punctuation. Don't prejudge ideas before you write them down. Just write whatever comes to mind.

It might take a little bit to get the ideas flowing. First with some nonsense. Then some bad ideas. But eventually, some good ideas will start to pop. Or at least idea fragments on which you can build.

Here's what some of my free writing looks like, typos and all.

I am so freakin tired. I need coffee. But I gotta deadline coming up. How am I going to finish teh story? Shea's trying to stop Manfield. She doesn't know where he is. I don't know where he is. Where is Manfield hiding? Or is he hiding? Maybe he's just hard to get to. I don't know. I don't know. Ugh, this is boring.

Why can't I come up with any ideas? I feel like such a failure. My friends in the writers group never seem to have any problems coming up with ideas. What's wrong with me. Maybe I need to meditate or do affirmations. No, I'm doing freewriting. Okay, maybe Manfield has taken Shea's neice hostage. Yeah, I like that idea. And he contacts her and tells her to meet at the bridge over the river. Tells her to come alone. But she doesn't. She's gonna bring the Sisterhood with her. Gonna be a big fight.

No major lightning strikes of ideas. The process starts with me stuck in my head, struggling to focus on the story. But that's okay. Because then I start asking myself questions. Those questions trigger ideas. Not necessarily great ideas. But little somethings I can build on when I get back into the story.

I like to say that we can't wait for our muse to show up. We can't wait to be "in the flow" before we start writing. The flow happens after we've been writing a while.

If the good ideas aren't flowing, then we go with the bad ideas. As we write out the bad ideas, better ideas will start to rise into our consciousness. And then even better ideas. And occasional strokes of genius.

The act of writing attracts our muse, not the quality of the writing. Eventually, she will show up and say, "Here, try this instead." She won't come at our beck and call. But we can lure her when we simply do the work and write.

Putting the Tools into Practice

You can use all of these tools, or some of them, or none of them. Your choice entirely. Our goal is to gradually change our relationship to our writing and ourselves as creatives.

At one time, writing was fun for us, a labor of love. Then it became hard. We started taking it seriously. Maybe a little too seriously. Writing became work. Resentments crept in. And what was fun was no longer fun.

We can make it fun again. We can use the tools that work for us, that help us dismantle the negativity and self-doubts that plague us.

We can be intentional about falling back in love with writing and enjoy the aspects of the creative process that have lost their luster. And we can learn to appreciate the effort that we put into each story we tell.

7

Healthy Body, Healthy Mind, Healthy Muse

Overcoming creative self-doubt requires more than a few coping mechanisms and therapeutic tools. We need a holistic approach. Meditation and affirmations produce better results when we aren't neglecting our basic self-care. We get more out of journaling and gratitude lists when we take care of our bodies and minds.

Exercise

Okay, now I know a lot of readers are scratching their heads, wondering why I'm bringing up exercise in a book about self-doubt and creativity. I get it. I really do.

Others of you are experiencing a myriad of feelings related to body-shaming just from the word "exercise." Don't worry. I'm not here to tell you to lose weight. Or gain weight. This isn't about your body shape.

But science has shown that regular exercise makes our

brains work more efficiently. It optimizes the biochemistry. And while I am a far cry from being an athlete by any definition, I have discovered that going for a walk or a run a few times a week helps me deal with those demons of self-doubt while also sparking my creativity.

Sure, exercise is that awful thing your doctor is always harping on you to do more of. Mine too. I'm 5' 6" and weigh nearly two hundred pounds. So I get it.

And I'm not recommending exercise for everyone. Check with your doctor before beginning any new exercise regimen. Seriously, I don't want you to drop dead from a heart attack, especially if you're out of shape like I am.

Here's the deal. Exercise stimulates the release of endorphins, dopamine, norepinephrine, and serotonin. These neurotransmitters will boost your mood, help you sleep better, and improve your appetite. Ultimately, they will help push that little negativity troll back into the basement where it belongs. Sure, you may be fatigued and barely able to move after a good workout, but emotionally, you'll feel better.

Exercise is a great way to get out of your head and focus your mind on the physical sensations of your body moving and your breath moving in and out of your lungs. It's like a physical version of meditation.

From my own experience (and again, I don't exercise nearly as much as I should), it helps me work through issues like when a scene is giving me trouble. Exercise can keep the inner critic distracted enough that ideas bubble up. Just something about the movement, the sunshine, my heart pounding and sending more oxygen to my brain. It truly helps.

When I exercise, I usually alternate walking with short bursts of jogging. But keep in mind I'm an overweight, middle-aged woman. With your doctor's approval, do what speaks to you, whether it's bicycling, swimming, Pilates, dancing, or any other aerobic routine. Just get your body moving a few times a week.

If all you can do is sit in a chair and do leg lifts for five minutes, that's okay. It will still produce results. Start with where you are and do what you can to give your body a boost.

Sleep

I mentioned above how exercise can help you sleep. I bring it up because getting a proper amount of sleep is crucial for creativity.

When you are sleep-deprived, your body doesn't function nearly as well. Neither does your mind. The creativity well dries up.

A lack of sleep can adversely affect your mood, sabotaging your defenses against your inner troll. You doubt and second-guess everything you write. And considering how sleep deprivation can sap your cognitive functions, your little troll may be right, to an extent. You write better when you've had a good night's sleep.

We all have different sleep cycles and need varying amounts of sleep. My wife has always had a crazy sleep cycle and can function on a few hours of sleep at night. But then she might take a few naps during the day. She's retired, and that works for her.

Me? I need a good eight to nine hours of sleep to function. I'm not much of a day napper. I go to bed early and get up early. But that's my body's natural rhythm. Whether you're an early bird like me or a night owl like my wife, pay attention to what your body is telling you.

When you get the proper amount of sleep, it will be like a power boost to your muse and inner editor while silencing the troll.

Hydration and Proper Diet

Your body and mind need fuel to operate efficiently. That means drinking enough water and eating a healthy diet.

Again, I am not telling you to lose weight. Okay? So relax. You're beautiful and amazing no matter your body shape or BMI or any of that nonsense.

But if you're living on caffeine and snack foods and not drinking enough water, you're risking a burnout.

I live in the desert. Hydration is key to survival. It is also important to keep the old brain functioning. Water is to the body and mind what oil is to a car engine. Without it, things don't work so well.

Caffeinated drinks, sodas, and alcohol are okay in moderation, but you need to get most of your hydration from good ol' dihydrogen monoxide (aka H_2O, aka water).

Getting enough water improves not only your ability to write but also your mood, keeping the nasty old troll at bay.

The same applies to food. If water is the motor oil, food is the fuel. If all you eat is junk food, it's like putting bad gasoline in the tank of your car. It might run for a while, but you'll soon be running into major problems and costly repairs.

Snack foods are okay in moderation. I love ice cream and beef jerky and biscotti and many unhealthful foods. No shame. But to get the most out of your writing time, be sure to have some lean proteins, veggies, and fruit.

I want to emphasize once again, I am not here to shame you with any of these suggestions, okay? I am not telling you to lose weight or stop eating junk food. Simply be aware of how your nutrition can affect your ability to create. Be open to making minor improvements.

Helping Others

I'm sure you're thinking, "Whew! I'm glad she's stopped harping about exercise and eating better. But what does helping others have to do with overcoming creative self-doubt?"

It's a good question. I have a good answer.

Helping others is another great way to get out of our own heads. Like gratitude lists, this practice changes the direction of our thinking from negative to positive. And if we're halfway decent people, we enjoy helping people.

With writing, we can help people by participating in a critique group and offering constructive feedback. We can offer to be beta readers for fellow writers.

One way I've found to help people is to be a sensitivity reader. More people are including transgender characters. But a lot of cisgender (non-trans) authors aren't familiar with what life is like as a trans person. They know general things but not the more complex issues. They are unfamiliar with how we use language to describe our experiences.

But these authors, generally speaking, want to write authentic trans characters. So they hire someone like me to read through their work, point out potentially harmful issues (that could result in blowback against them), and suggest how to write a more authentic representation of my community and tell a better story.

There are myriad ways to help other writers. Volunteering with writer organizations or at conferences can be helpful and educational. Sharing your knowledge in writer groups on social media can also be helpful to them and you.

Not only does helping other writers make you feel better about yourself, but it fosters that sense of connection and community, reminding you that you are not alone on this journey. We are all in this together. We all need help from time to time. We all have doubts. Together, we can work through them.

Forgiveness

"It's as if a million voices suddenly cried out in terror and were suddenly silenced." Okay, maybe I exaggerate, but I know some of you are doing some serious eye rolling about now. Sleep and exercise? Okay, fine. But forgiveness? Yeah, not what you expected, huh? What's to forgive? Who should you forgive? And why?

Let's start with forgiving yourself for not being the writer you think you should be. When the fun of writing turned into work, some resentments crept into your mind. Yes? And maybe you directed some of those resentments at yourself for not being smarter or more talented or not having an MFA or whatever excuse you're using to blame yourself for being human, just like the rest of us poor schlubs.

Maybe you also have resentments against others. Resentments against certain teachers for not being more supportive mentors. Resentments against your folks for all myriad offenses (been there, got the therapy T-shirt). Resentments against an agent or publisher for not accepting your submission. Resentments against a peer for getting that award or *NY Times* review or bestseller status that you felt you deserved.

I'm not saying you don't have a right to feel resentments. The question is, do you want the baggage and consequences that those resentments carry with them?

If someone harmed you, forgiving them doesn't mean what they did was okay. You're not letting them off the hook for what they did. You're letting yourself off the hook, by freeing yourself of having to continue to relive the trauma and the ways it holds you back, robbing you of the peace of mind you deserve.

Forgiveness means that you recognize you have a resentment against yourself, another person, or life, and that you're choosing to free your mind of that burden. Forgiveness is simply choosing not to let it harm you any more in the future. It's a conscious choice to let go of the toxic negativity of resentments.

You are choosing peace and gentleness rather than bitterness, shame, and anger. Negativity and resentments empower your troll. They give it ammunition, robbing you of your creativity. You may have a right to feel angry. But you also have a right to let it go and no longer let it dominate your mind and block your creative juices.

We all wish we were better writers than we are. And if we continue to write and work on our craft, we will become better writers than we are now. Eventually, we will get our skills to where we want them to be. For the time being, though, maybe we should cut ourselves a break.

Don't use a lack of formal education as an excuse to hate on yourself ("I should have gone to college" or "I should have earned an MFA"). Don't use your actual education as a reason to hate on yourself either ("I spent all this money on a degree in writing, and I can't finish this novel").

Stop hating yourself for not being perfect. Because you know what they say about "perfect"? Perfect is the enemy of good.

In Alcoholics Anonymous, we have a slogan, "Progress, not perfection." If we can do a little better today than we did yesterday or last month, then we're making progress, and that's a good thing. But if we start shaming ourselves for not being perfect, that shame won't help the situation. More likely, it will just make it worse. It will certainly make us feel worse. And we don't want that. We don't deserve that.

So next time you feel ashamed of your writing, make a conscious choice to let yourself off the hook. It's probably a lot better than you think it is, anyway.

Stop hating others for where you are now. Yes, some of them were assholes who treated you horribly in the past. Don't treat yourself horribly by continuing to traumatize yourself by letting them live rent-free in your head. The best revenge is living well, and that starts by choosing peace for yourself.

Stop resenting fellow authors for their success. Sure, we wish we won that award or got that six-figure publishing deal they scored, even if they aren't half the writer we are. But so what? Keep writing. Do it for the love of the writing. Eventually, someone will notice.

Tell yourself, "I'm ready to let go of this shame and resentment. I'm ready to embrace myself as a writer, with whatever skills I have right now, knowing that I will continue to improve over time. I'm ready to celebrate my awesome author journey rather than obsess over someone else's. I'm ready to prove that negative creative writing teacher wrong. I'm ready to succeed despite what any agent or publisher decides."

When you read something you wrote a few years ago and it's not nearly as good as something you wrote last month, realize that's a good thing. It means you're getting better as a writer. It's something to be proud of. To be grateful for. You're making progress. Forgive the writer you were, knowing that you have improved. Forgive those in your past. Use the trauma as fodder for your stories.

8

Understanding Your Creative Process

Creation is messy. Write that sentence on your bathroom mirror. Tattoo it on your forearm. Brand it onto your soul. Okay, maybe pass on the tattoo.

The point is that you internalize and accept that the creative process is messy. You may have to shift gears and try new things along the way. If you get stuck, you may have to switch to writing longhand until you get your groove back. Or write in a different location or at a different time of day.

You may have to outline a few scenes if you don't already have an outline. If you do have an outline, you may need to change it. Or even write without the outline for a bit.

Creation is an iterative process. That means you don't get it all perfect in a single attempt. Sculptors rough out the basic shapes before they work on the fine details. Painters may lay in broad swaths of color for the background before anything on the canvas looks like what it's supposed to be.

In writing, we may or may not outline. Then we write a rough draft to get a basic feel for where the story is going and what are characters are like. Then we go back through and address plot holes and pare down info dumps. We polish the dialogue and replace the dull nouns and verbs with stronger ones. We cut out our overly used crutch words. We go back over it and over the story, revising and refining, until it is as good as we can make it.

Creating is an organic process that produces unique results every time. We're not manufacturing widgets. We're not telling the same story over and over again.

Every book or poem or short story we write is something completely new, even if we're using the same characters from a previous story and roughly the same process or structure.

We aren't sure what the finished product will look like. There are no guarantees in how reviewers or readers will respond to it. This uncertainty is at the heart of our fear and self-doubt, but it is also part of the excitement.

If you're like most creatives, you're always trying to improve your skills. You try alternative approaches, experiment with new tools, push boundaries, and take chances. Create new worlds, fresh adventures, unique challenges, new twists, and other points of view. Because you have to keep the reader engaged, wondering what will happen next.

A common question we writers are asked is whether we are plotters or pantsers. In other words, do we outline before we write the rough draft, or do we plunge straight into the drafting process without an outline and discover the story as we go?

That question has no right or wrong answer. I find a lot of authors start one way with one project, then try another way with the next project, and end up somewhere in the middle a few projects later.

I consider myself a hybrid. I will create a rough outline, enough to give me a basic idea of where I want to take the story. But I'm not married to that outline. If I'm going along in the drafting process and I come up with a better idea for where I am in the story, I'll go with the better idea.

My outline may tell me that my bounty hunter shows up at the fugitive's house, but she doesn't find him. But what if she finds him, they fight, and he gets away? That could be a more exciting scene. That's what I'll go with. Tell the better story.

And let's get real about rough drafts. They're rough. They're supposed to be rough. They're not shitty. They're not awful. They're just rough. They give us a basic idea of where the story is going. And we are free to change it.

The dialogue may be clunky. Your characters may be one-dimensional. The narration may be chock-full of weak nouns, dull verbs, and cheesy adverbs. Characters may do an inordinate amount of nodding or smiling or sighing. Filler words like "just" and "some" may have invaded your draft like a swarm of termites. But that's okay. It's only one step in the process.

Your rough draft is unpolished because you haven't polished it yet. It's exactly what it's supposed to be at this stage of the messy creative process. So don't start with all of that trash talk about how awful it is. You wouldn't say that when critiquing another writer's early draft. Be nice to yourself.

Don't compare your rough draft to someone else's published novel. That's ridiculous for multiple reasons. If you saw their rough draft, it might surprise you how rough theirs is.

Yes, there are a few rare people like Dean Martin Smith who can create a clean, perfect novel in one fell swoop. But the guy's written a gazillion novels. Let's not compare ourselves with him. It's not a fair comparison.

For all its flaws, your rough draft is full of all kinds of good stuff, like rough diamonds that must be cut for people to see their brilliance. Storylines and subplots and characters and descriptions that, with some work, will eventually shine and enthrall your readers.

Remember that every published novel started out as a rough draft. Lines had to be rewritten countless times. Entire scenes were cut. Characters were merged with others or done away with entirely or completely reworked.

I once discovered that I had five distinct characters with the name Michael in the rough draft of *Iron Goddess*. I do not know why. In the same book, I had too many characters whose last names started with *S*.

If your rough draft doesn't shine like a flawless diamond, don't worry about it. You will fix it later. This is part of the creative process. It's messy. It's iterative. Learn to trust the process. Learn to trust *your* process. Adapt as you need to. Adapting and developing are part of your process.

You also need to understand that different parts of the process require different skill sets and different parts of your brain. Outlining and drafting are ninety-five percent creative juice (think "muse") with minimal critical thinking needed. When drafting, keep your inner editor locked up in a closet and gagged with a sock in their mouth. This is muse territory. This is the time to play "what if?" Time to play and take chances, try crazy new things, throw shit at the wall and see what sticks.

Don't be afraid to write yourself into a corner. Getting stuck means you're taking chances. Impossible situations will get the reader emotionally invested. How's our intrepid investigator going to get out of this mess? How will our heroine and hero ever fall back in love? It seems impossible. But this apparent impossibility gives your story the tension it needs to keep the reader reading. You'll figure it out.

Take some time to brainstorm and freewrite. I have to do this frequently. I will write my protagonist into a no-win situation. And then I may take a day or more to puzzle out a solution. Or several solutions.

If freewriting doesn't get you stuck, try something different. Try writing at a different location or time of day. Write on a different device or by hand. Give dictating a try. Write a character interview. Watch some old TV shows and make notes on the plot devices they're using. Go for a run or shoot some hoops. Read some old paperbacks collecting dust on your shelves. Take a little break. Or take a big break.

Again, the creative process is messy. Just as the early American pioneers often ran into obstacles like mountains and deep gorges and fast-moving rivers, forcing them to backtrack and try alternative routes or methods in their journey westward, you will have to shift gears every so often to reach your destination.

Sometimes, sideways or backward is the only way forward. You may have to make some adjustments earlier in the story for a solution that makes sense. This is often how authors insert red herrings and foreshadowing into a story. You don't have to do it in the rough draft, but maybe make a note to revisit it when you revise.

Pay as much attention to what's going on inside you as what's ending up on the page. Emotions play a big part in the writing process. Use the tools provided earlier in this book to work through feelings of resistance, self-doubt, and fear.

Once you've completed the rough draft, give yourself some time to celebrate your accomplishment. Pop some champagne. Chow down on a celebratory pizza! Order that latest *Star Wars* action figure you've had your eye on. You deserve it.

Some writers put away their first draft for a few weeks so that they don't get too close to the story. Not a bad idea. A little distance and objectivity can help when you begin the revision process. Or if you'd rather jump right back in, like I tend to do, that's okay too.

This is your creative process. You get to do it however

you want to do it. You can try one approach and, if it works, continue to do it that way. If it doesn't, try something else and see if that works better.

My process is ever evolving. I've written eight novels so far. My process has been different (sometimes *very* different) with each one. Sometimes, I will outline an entire novel before I write the first scene. Other times, I will just let the story evolve, writing organically (or "by the seat of my pants") until I get to a point where I get stuck and need to outline the next few scenes or the rest of the book. I may go back and forth.

The revision process is unsurprisingly more analytical than the drafting process. You can release your inner editor from that dark closet and take off the gag. Crack your knuckles and break out the red pens.

But be gentle with yourself. Don't shame yourself or your work. The purpose of revising isn't to focus on how imperfect your rough draft is. That doesn't help. Just look for ways to improve the story.

The inner editor's job is to take what your muse has created and transform it to tell the best story you can. With each pass, you will make it better. Each story you write will be a little better than the one before.

Allow the muse to chime in from time to time too. There's still a lot of creativity in the revision process. It's okay to continue experimenting with scenes and characters, especially on a first revision.

But now you're paying more attention to story structure, character development, and word usage. Your rough draft has given you a framework that you now refine.

You don't have to fix everything at once. Again, this process is iterative. There are no hard-and-fast rules about how many drafts you need to go through. A good rule of thumb is to start broad and work your way in. Don't worry so much about the typos the first few times through as the bigger issues such as plot holes, continuity errors, and story structure.

On the first revision, a lot of authors go through the rough draft and just make notes. No changes. The goal is to get an overview of what needs work. This can spark ideas. New plot twists. New dimensions to your characters. Even a new ending.

Once you've fixed the major structural issues, you can focus on subtler issues such as character development, narrative voice, POV shifts, and dialogue on subsequent drafts. Again, not all at once. Focus on one thing at a time.

You may also continue to discover big issues you missed the first time. Or you may fix one issue only to cause problems somewhere else in the story. It happens. Sometimes it feels like trying to solve a Rubik's cube. Don't worry. You'll figure it out.

Revision doesn't have to be drudge work. Don't get me wrong—it's hard work. Sometimes it can get a little boring and repetitive. It can feel like punishment.

But it's not punishment. It simply takes a different energy, a different part of the brain. You are shifting gears. And sometimes, this shift can be hard to make.

Here, a willingness to see things differently really comes into play. Be willing to see the creative aspect of revision. Be willing to see the joy in improving on what you've written.

When we find a section of our story that isn't working, we can be creative in our approach to restructuring. We can brainstorm ideas. Move sentences around. Try a completely different way to describe something in the scene. Look at it from different perspectives. What might ramp up the tension? Or reveal deeper, possibly contradictory aspects of a character's nature?

I have learned a lot about my ever-evolving creative process by listening to other authors talk about their processes. I learn about alternative approaches, techniques, and perspectives.

As mentioned, there are some people who can create a polished manuscript in a single draft. And there are people who need to go back over it a thousand times. There are people who can write a full novel in a week. And there are others who take years.

Because writing is a craft that requires us to master so many unique skills, and each of us comes to writing with different innate talents and experiences, there is no right or wrong way to get the job done.

Whenever I stall on a project, when that beginning energy wanes (as it often does about a third of the way through the story), I allow myself to consider different ways to push through.

Would reworking my outline help me get my groove back? Should I forget the outline and start writing organically, letting the characters and the plot go where they seem to want? Do I need to lie down for a while in a semi-lucid state and brainstorm possibilities?

Again, no wrong answers. Anything that gets me back in the seat writing again is a good thing. Even if later, I scrap what I'm writing. Scrapping a line, a paragraph, even an entire chapter in favor of something better doesn't mean that I've wasted any time. I had to write the not-so-great version of a scene before I discovered the amazing version of the scene. The not-so-great version gave me something to riff off of, a springboard to help me reach greatness. And that is always time well spent.

I personally have trouble working on a new project after I've just launched the previous one. It's not simply that I'm blocked or out of ideas. But sometimes it takes me a while to shift gears in my brain from launching one book into writing the rough draft of the next one.

Some people can work on the rough draft of a new story

in the morning then switch gears and work on revising a different story in the afternoon. Or switch to marketing or publishing or some other related activity that requires very different energy. If that's you, fantastic. But if not, that's okay.

Learn how your brain works. I like focusing on one project at a time. Other people like to work on multiple projects at various stages. Figure out what works best for you. We figure it out by trying it one way, and then if that doesn't work, trying it another way.

Some writers dread getting edits back from an editor. Others dread book launches. Still others hate having to market their books, writing blurbs and other forms of sales copy, appearing at live events, interacting on social media, being interviewed on podcasts, etc. Some of us are introverts. Others are extroverts. We each derive joy from different parts of this process.

We are all discovering and modifying our process. And as I said, the process is messy. Whenever you get stuck or feel a strong resistance to wherever you are in your writing/editing/publishing process, pay attention to what's going on inside of you.

Try changing something. Try a different approach. Re-center your mind. Remind yourself of the reasons you love being an author. Remember why you dreamed of becoming an author. If you need to, take a break from it. Feed your creative self.

Recently, I was launching a novel at the same time that I was supposed to be writing the rough draft of the next novel. But despite creating an outline for the story quickly, I struggled to write the opening scene. My inner editor escaped her bonds and kept nitpicking everything. *This scene isn't exciting enough. Do I really need this character? Does this paragraph advance the story?* My energy was scattered.

I realized that I needed to hold off writing that novel.

I'd come back to it. I still love the story I will tell. But I'm not ready to tell it. Not while much of my mind is focused on launching the previous novel. Some people can multitask like that. Not me. It diffuses my mental energy so much that I struggle with the tasks I should be doing.

So I set that new novel aside while I focused on the book launch. And then I started a different project. I also did something else. I adjusted my production schedule so that I'm no longer overlapping projects like that.

Pay attention when something isn't working for you in your process. Consider your options. Do you need to slow down? Take a break? Even if it means pushing a deadline, sometimes you have to do it. As much as we love being authors, we have to take care of our physical and mental health. Otherwise, we risk burnout or major health problems.

The next time you run into problems or find you're avoiding writing or revising or any of the tasks you need to do to put out your next novel, ask yourself, "How can I see this differently? What is my mind trying to tell me? What is my body trying to tell me? What about this stage of this process is troubling me? What do I need to change to reach the next stage for this project or my writing career?"

The answers are inside of you because your authorial process is unique to you. Your combination of talents, skills, perception, beliefs, and experiences makes you the unique author that you are. That blend gives you a unique voice. Listen to it. And be gentle. No shaming yourself for not meeting a daily writing goal or an editorial deadline or even a launch date. Love yourself through this process.

Does it help to write and edit and work on other aspects of your books at the same place and time every day? Or is it easier to change things up and work in a different environment? If you always write at a desk in your home, maybe try writing on a couch in another room or at a cafe.

Sometimes we have to remove distractions. Sometimes we have to add them. Sounds crazy, but changing the writing environment can have a positive effect for some writers.

Do you write better with music, white noise, or dead silence? I listen to different types of music depending on what I'm writing or editing. If I'm writing an action sequence, the energy of certain movie soundtracks or EDM can get me excited and the words flowing. If I'm writing a deeply emotional scene, maybe classical or angelic choir music. Other times, it's atmospheric New Age music or blues or classic jazz.

Look at your routine. Are you a morning writer? An afternoon writer? Or an evening writer? Often, our lives dictate our writing schedules, forcing us to make choices. Would it be better if you wrote early in the morning before anyone else got up? Or late at night after the kids were asleep? Maybe you take public transportation and have little choice but to learn to write on your mobile phone or by hand. Look at your options.

Also consider whether you're the kind of writer who needs to be reminded to take breaks. Utilizing a timer (be it on an electronic device or a clock) may help you make best use of the time and avoid wasting hours watching cat videos on YouTube videos or doomscrolling on Twitter.

Dividing a colossal task into twenty-five-minute chunks (or whatever time interval works best), especially an unpleasant one, can help you power through.

Sometimes a section of story I'm writing fills me with strong emotions. I throw myself deeply into the minds of my characters to the point of crying while writing a death scene or feeling a sense of dread during an "all is lost" moment. Sometimes, the story triggers a personal past trauma. Getting it out onto the page is cathartic but also exhausting.

Pacing myself while writing and editing these kinds of

scenes is an absolute must for me. Write for a quick sprint, then take a break and decompress.

It's also important for me to get my body moving and boost the old circulation. Not such a big deal when I was younger, but now that I'm in my mid-fifties, I have to do it to avoid my ankles from swelling.

Bottom line is we have to pay attention to the wheres and whens and hows of our creative process. We have to be open to possibilities and change things up when we get stuck. We have to pay attention to our mental and physical health.

Trust the process. Trust *your* process.

9

Focus on the Work, Not the Results

As authors, there are things we can control and things we cannot. All too often, we try to manipulate people and situations beyond our control, which inevitably leads to frustration, anger, and all sorts of problems.

At the same time, we're neglecting the aspects of our author journey that we can control because we're too busy banging our heads against the wall trying to play puppet master.

In Alcoholics Anonymous, we regularly recite the Serenity Prayer. If you're not familiar with it, it goes like this:

God,
Grant me the serenity to accept the things I cannot change,
The courage to change the things I can,
And the wisdom to know the difference.

If you don't believe in God or a Higher Power, don't freak out on me. I'm not sharing this to convince you to believe in some metaphysical being.

Alcoholics and codependents like myself are notorious for trying to control the people around us (usually to everyone's detriment) while eschewing our own responsibilities. It's the nature of the disease.

To be honest, many of us authors aren't much better. We complain when someone gives our new release a one-star review or when sales tank suddenly. We bang our heads on our desks when we receive one rejection after another from agents or publishers. We berate ourselves for not meeting word count goals. And we spiral into a depression when our friends win awards while our work doesn't even get nominated.

Meanwhile, we waste time on social media when we could be writing. We get lost down the rabbit hole of research long past the point where we are learning useful information. Yes, I see you watching cat videos under the guise of research.

We obsess over making sure we have the right playlist to listen to while writing or complain that our favorite coffeehouse isn't open because of COVID restrictions. We don't bother learning how to write a proper pitch for a query letter or book description when that is key to signing an agent or converting readers on Amazon.

We need to pay attention to the aspects of our author journey and creative process where we are trying to control things over which we have no control. We need to take responsibility for the things we can control.

Having the wisdom to know the difference between the two is key to having not only a successful author career but a joyful one as well. And that's what we will look at.

Bottom line is we control our choices, attitudes, and actions, but not the results. We can only control the work and our process but not the specific outcome. Seth Godin talks a lot about this in his book *The Practice*. If you haven't read it, I highly recommend doing so.

We can control what we write. We get to choose the genre and the length of our stories. We can choose to change genres at any time. However, and this is a big caveat, we cannot control how many of our readers will follow us from one genre to the next.

If we're writing military sci-fi and we decide we want to switch to urban fantasy for our next series, a significant portion of our fans will not make the leap with us. It doesn't matter how clever you are at marketing or persuading.

Readers tend to be genre loyal and even series loyal. My wife *loves* Faith Hunter's Jane Yellowrock series about a professional vampire hunter. But she refused to jump to Hunter's other series. Same with Jim Butcher's books. She adores his Dresden series but has no interest in his Codex Alera or Cinder Spire series.

Readers read in the genres they love because the tropes in those genres speak to them in a way that other genres do not. Romance readers insist on a happy-ever-after ending. It's nonnegotiable. So if you write romance but publish a story without an HEA, you will piss off a lot of your followers. They will abandon you like rats from a sinking ship, leaving a slew of one-star reviews in their wake.

Genre-hop all you want, but accept the consequences of doing so. Don't attempt to control your existing fans. Don't respond to negative reviews from fans who don't like what you're writing now. You can't control them. Don't even try.

You can control how you brand yourself. If you write in multiple genres, you can write under one name in one genre and under a different pen name (even if it's adding an initial like I did with this book) in the other. You will probably separate your marketing for followers of each genre (including separate newsletters).

More work? Yes. But you will have a much more positive response from each subset of followers.

This brings me to the gray areas. More specifically, those situations over which we have no control but do have influence. In these situations, we can do things to optimize results, even if we cannot force a specific outcome.

When it comes to the writing process itself, we can control when, where, and for how long we sit down and write. We cannot necessarily control how many words we write in a given session.

You may want to write two thousand words in a twenty-five-minute writing sprint. But many factors could affect that outcome. You could write yourself into a corner. Maybe you're tired. You may have a cold. That argument you had with your spouse could be buzzing in the back of your mind. Put in the time and let the word count take care of itself.

We can make choices to optimize our daily word counts. We can get up early and write. We can make it part of our routine to shut off social media or internet access when we should be writing. Emphasis on "making it part of our routine." Just doing it once in a while doesn't help.

We can notice the habits we've fallen into that derail our productivity and are nothing but stall tactics like obsessing over which playlist we listen to while we write. We can make sure we get a proper amount of sleep and stay hydrated, maximizing our mental and creative juices.

In the area of publishing, we can control which literary agents or publishers we submit to. We cannot control whether a specific publisher or agent will sign us. Our odds, on average, are less than one percent. No kidding. I submitted to ninety agents before I signed with mine.

Again, we can do things to improve our chances, such as studying how to write a proper query letter. I highly recommend Query Shark (https://queryshark.blogspot.com/) to learn how to write query letters. But once we send the query, the control is out of our hands. We simply have to let go and focus on writing the next book.

If we're going the self-publishing route, we can control

a lot of things, such as which retailers and distributors we use to publish our books. We can control which formats we publish in. We can control how we market our work. We can learn how to write book blurbs that convert (I highly recommend the *Blurbs Sell Books* podcast).

We cannot control how many books we sell. We cannot control whether BookBub accepts us for a Featured Deal. We cannot even control whether Amazon suddenly decides to discount our paperbacks. Trust me, complaining does no good.

We can control how well edited our books are by hiring professional editors, but we cannot control how critics and readers will review our books. All books get at least some one-star reviews. The ones that don't have any one- or two-star reviews rarely have many reviews in the first place.

We can control which awards we submit our books to, but we can't control whether we are finalists or winners.

All of these points may seem obvious, but so many of us spend an inordinate amount of time trying to control that which we can't. This can lead to frustration when we don't get the results we want, and that can further lead to resentments toward ourselves and the people we work with.

I've seen writers express frustration at their inability to write a certain number of words a day or sell a certain number of books per month or win awards or get the reviews they seek. Hey, I get it. I've been there.

Some go so far as to rage against agents for refusing to sign them, or they'll reply to one-star reviews trying to explain to the reviewer they're wrong. Both are spectacularly bad ideas and can sink your career. Word gets around about unacceptable behavior like this.

Don't get distracted by things outside of your control or influence. When disappointment comes (and it will, many times), let yourself feel the emotions, then let them go and get back to work.

10

The Middle Way

Remember those early days when you were a newbie author with visions of becoming the next Ernest Hemingway or Toni Morrison or Agatha Christie or Danielle Steel or Isaac Asimov? The possibilities were endless.

You were going to be the next rising star, the wunderkind. The fresh literary voice that would change the world.

You'd sign a six-figure deal with one of the Big Five publishers and go on a worldwide book-signing tour. You'd get glowing reviews from the *New York Times* and appear on *Late Night with Stephen Colbert* and *Fresh Air with Terry Gross*.

I'm sure you remember the excitement and exhilaration. You wrote without fear, without worrying about rules. You wrote for the pure joy of it. It was fun creating characters, inventing worlds and telling exciting, ever-twisting stories. Even if it was fan fiction in which Sam Winchester fell in love with Castiel, or Bella from *Twilight* teamed up with Buffy the Vampire Slayer.

It didn't matter that your stories didn't fit the traditional story structure or that your dialogue was clunky or that your prose was as purple as a new bruise. You loved doing it. You loved playing "what if" in your imaginary worlds.

And then you got your first critique. Maybe it was from a fellow fledgling writer, a teacher, or a professional editor. The red ink on your pristine pages felt like it had spattered from a dagger jammed deep into your heart.

You realized in that moment that you weren't the wunderkind you thought you were. That your perfect prose wasn't so perfect. That you were breaking all kinds of rules, telling where you should have been showing, throwing in adverbs like they were grains of salt to shore up your weak nouns and verbs.

Suddenly, you felt awful. Your work was crap. Writing was no longer a joyful experiment with endless possibilities. Now it was hard, a boring chore with countless rules to follow. And just when you thought you understood all of them, someone would throw more at you. Comma splices and misplaced modifiers and split infinitives and compound adverbial phrases.

You felt shame when anyone read your work. Rereading your own work was an exercise in humiliation that absolutely crushed your soul and left you wondering why you bothered.

The belief that your writing is all that and a bag of chips or that it is worse than cat vomit are examples of extreme thinking. We've all been there. I see it daily from fellow authors on social media, most of whom feel like imposters despite the accolades they've received.

Getting over the belief that your writing is all that and a bag of chips isn't usually a problem. It is a delusion that is soon shattered when we get feedback from other writers or editors. Though I have known a few holdouts—newbies who were absolutely convinced of the divine perfection of even their roughest drafts.

The disillusionment that comes from realizing our work

isn't perfect can be painful. It can stop some of us from ever writing again, especially if the person giving the critique isn't mindful of the fledgling writer's feelings. The feedback we get from fellow writers and editors is nothing compared to the vicious reviews that readers leave online. Have you stopped by Goodreads lately? It's a bloodbath!

The challenge then lies in the other extreme. Many of us are so traumatized by the realization of how imperfect our work is that we become convinced it will always be so. That no amount of revising or improving our craft will make us anything but a hack and a fraud. Even if our work garners praise from major reviewers, becomes a *New York Times* bestseller, and wins awards, this extremely negative view toward our work can metastasize into viewing ourselves as a fraud. We feel like an imposter.

"Sure, this book won a Nebula Award or received a glowing review in the *L.A. Times*, but it's a fluke. I'm not nearly as talented as they think I am. My next book will flop. And when it does, everyone will hate me. They will see me as the hack that I am. They will take back my awards. Publishers will cancel my contracts. Amazon will ban me for life."

Writers are not unique in struggling with imposter syndrome. A lot of successful creatives face this toxic form of extreme thinking. We are terrified of whatever success we've experienced. The uncertain and inexact nature of creativity feels like we're swimming in quicksand. We're afraid of backlash. We will dismiss any positive feedback as delusional while obsessing over the one-star ratings and scorching reviews.

Do people in less creative professions suffer this level of insecurity? Do doctors and lawyers wake up in cold sweats, worrying that the powers that be will take away their license to practice? Do architects and IT managers feel like imposters? Does an A/C technician fear losing his certification? Maybe they do. I don't know. I do know that many writers and other creatives do.

The good news is we don't have to be writers who abhor our work, who are afraid of success, who are so immobilized by self-doubt that we become blocked and sabotage our careers. There is an alternative.

In Buddhism, the concept of the Middle Way offers a relief between two extremes. The Middle Way isn't some mind-blowing concept. The Middle Way helps us recognize extreme thinking and its flaws while finding a path of moderation instead.

The Buddha Siddhartha Gautama grew up as a prince in extreme wealth and privilege. So much so that when he finally saw how most people lived and, more importantly, how they suffered, became ill, and died, he walked away from his privilege.

Initially, he became an ascetic, denying himself all sensual pleasures. No relaxing. No playful activities. No joy. Just sitting and meditating all day, every day. Eating and drinking just enough to sustain life and nothing more. He became emaciated like his teachers. He pursued this extreme self-denial, hoping to attain spiritual enlightenment and ending humanity's suffering.

But his asceticism didn't produce enlightenment and wisdom. It didn't end the world's suffering, only added to his own. The Buddha's enlightenment came after he walked away from the extremes of asceticism.

It is said that a woman named Sujata offered him a bowl of kheer, a milk-rice pudding. The Buddha realized that neither extreme indulgence nor extreme self-denial brought him the answers he sought. He found the path to enlightenment in moderation between the two.

While you may not be seeking to end the world's suffering through spiritual enlightenment, understanding the Middle Way can help you in your creative work. Neither the extreme attitude that you're the greatest writer who ever lived nor that your work is garbage will provide you with the joy and satisfaction you seek from your writing.

The Middle Way is broad. Our work may not be the most amazing collection of words ever written, but neither is it the worst. It is somewhere in the middle. There is no way to pinpoint exactly where in the middle, because everyone who reads it will have a different opinion. It's not a mathematical equation with a quantifiable solution.

Our work may inspire one reader who loves it so much they binge-read everything we've written to date and beg for more. The same stories may get brutally panned as blithering garbage by a different reader, often by someone who isn't our target reader or who has some other bias.

Some snobbish reviewers have a major bias against genre fiction, especially romance. Personally, I suspect many of them are failed novelists with axes to grind and MFA degrees gathering dust on their shelves. Don't give these shriveled mushrooms an ounce of consideration. Their opinions don't matter in the scheme of things.

How do we steer ourselves away from the extreme thinking of our work and ourselves as writers? How do we find the Middle Way? It starts with willingness. Yeah, there's that word again. We have to be willing to see ourselves differently. We have to be willing to see our work differently. We have to be willing to let go of our extreme thinking. We have to be willing to let go of what other people think of our work. That's not an easy thing to do sometimes.

It's okay if your troll responds with, "Nuh-uh. I'm not changing my mind about what kind of writer I am or what kind of drivel I write." A little resistance is normal. That's okay. Let it come.

Our goal isn't to force these new beliefs. We want to be gentle with ourselves. There may be a lot of trauma buried underneath all of this extreme negativity that may or may not have anything to do with our writing. Pay attention to what comes up. Be kind and tender with those wounded parts of ourselves.

Our goal is to look at our work and our writer selves honestly. In terms of the stages of an individual story, our rough drafts are going to be rough. They're supposed to be. They're not going to be like final drafts. They are the part of the process in which we explore ideas, plots, characters, etc. The words and scenes are more placeholders for when you go back and revise.

A revised draft is also imperfect. I go through three drafts or more before I send one to my copy editor and then to my proofreader. And even when it has gone through so many drafts and past so many other professionals' eyes, there may still be typos everyone missed. Because we are human. Because none of us are perfect.

I'm not suggesting you put out anything but the best book you possibly can. By all means, strive for excellence. Attend classes and read books (both on craft and in your genre) to hone your skills. Push the envelope and try things you're not sure you're ready to attempt. And if you're going the self-pub route like I do, hire the best editing team you can afford. Hire the best cover designer you can afford. Use the best formatting tools or hire a professional to create a professional-quality book.

If you're going the traditional publishing route, work with your agent and your publishing team to produce the best book you can. It's okay to push back on suggested edits and hold your ground if what you wrote tells your story better. Give input on cover design and other aspects where you're allowed. Don't be a diva, but be a team player.

Once that book is out in the wide world and in readers' hands, give yourself permission to love it, to be proud of it, knowing you gave it your all. Your all is good enough for where you are right now in your author's journey.

In terms of our careers, our second book will probably be better than our first book. It may or may not sell more copies, but it will be better. Our third book better than the first two. Because the more we write, the better we get. It may or may not make more money than previous efforts. Every career has its ups and downs. But overall, you will improve.

Don't get discouraged if the writing process doesn't seem to get easier. We are pushing ourselves to greater challenges with each story we write. Climbing a mountain can take the wind out of you no matter how many times you've done it. Writing a story, especially one that is as involved as a novel, is a challenging endeavor regardless of how many you've written.

When we look back on our earlier work, there is no need to shame ourselves that it isn't as good as our most recent work. If it's gone through a proper process of being edited and proofread by professionals, then it's not garbage. If it's garnering decent reviews, it's because your words are entertaining people.

I was recently rereading one of my older books to create a story bible for keeping track of characters, places, and things for future stories in the series. I found myself enjoying the story all over again. Not because it was all that and a bag of chips. There were the places I caught myself thinking, "I could reword this a little." But it's still a fun story.

Are there movies that you enjoy watching over and over? The more you watch them, the more you notice little imperfections. A continuity error. A minor plot hole. A place where a piece of lighting equipment or a camera is visible. But you still love the story and the characters.

That's what our earlier works can be. They may be

imperfect. We can see the imperfections more now than we could back then because we are wiser in the ways of storytelling. But we can still enjoy the story. We can still love the characters. We can be grateful for the readers who enjoyed it too. We can cherish the lessons we learned while writing it. We can feel good about our earlier works. We can find comfort in the Middle Way.

11

The Beginner's Mind

I didn't get serious about my writing until I was in my forties. Sure, I wrote some short stories when I was a teen. I had big dreams. I read *Writer's Digest* every month from cover to cover. I pored over the entries in *Writer's Market*, hoping to find a publisher for my work.

But it wasn't until after I'd won the National Novel Writing Month personal challenge decades later that I got serious about learning the craft of writing and all the skills I needed to master.

Like many of us when we start out, I was full of enthusiasm and very little knowledge about what made a good story. I dared to think I might even turn the literary world on its head with my revolutionary ideas and unique experiences to draw upon.

When I got a critique from an editor on my first novel, I felt like I'd been run through with a very dull sword. Skewered! Who knew there could be that much red ink on a page, much less three hundred pages!

After a few days of massaging my bruised ego, I began

using the feedback I'd received to learn the craft in earnest. I accepted that this was a part of the process of learning.

It was okay that I had made so many beginner mistakes. I was a beginner, after all. And I could correct the mistakes I had made. It was okay that I didn't know all the rules. I could learn them. It was okay that my characters were one-dimensional, my dialogue awkward, and my narration directionless. I was a student of the craft, and I would improve my mastery of all the skills required.

We all start out not knowing what we don't know. There are so many skills to master. It can feel overwhelming at times. Voice and tense and structure and character development and dialogue and description. How does one learn all of this?

If we're not careful, the reality of having so much to learn and the realization of how flawed our early efforts are can stifle our creativity altogether. We go to write a new story, but we're so worried about choosing the right tense, so determined not to spew out backstory in an info dump or head-hop from one character's perspective to another. We obsess over perfecting that first page, that first paragraph, that first sentence until we end up not writing a story at all.

This can happen not just when we're starting out but even after we've published a slew of books. You'd think that the more books you wrote, the easier it would get. But it never does. It just gets difficult at a different level.

We're not writing the same story over and over again. We are always breaking new ground, even if we are writing multiple books in a series with the same cast of characters. We are taking our characters in new directions, tackling new kinds of problems. We are constantly pushing ourselves to do better, write more strongly, pull the reader more deeply into our worlds.

So even if we are a veteran author, in many ways, we're

still a beginner. There is always something new to learn. More skills to hone and take to the next level.

It is helpful to adopt the Buddhist concept of the Beginner's Mind no matter where we are in our career.

When you were writing your first stories, your mind was open to the endless possibilities. You were passionate about writing and about learning the skills of the craft. You had no preconceptions. You didn't worry about the rules of writing. You didn't obsess over adverbs, info dumps, or POV shifts. You simply enjoyed writing.

That's the Beginner's Mind. Open, passionate, and without limits. You accept that there is a lot to learn. But that's not a burden. It's part of the joy and the journey. It's an adventure.

You accept that you will make mistakes because beginners make mistakes. It's not like we're performing surgery or building rockets. No one (except maybe a character) is going to die if we write awkward dialogue. Nothing is going to explode if we accidentally start head-hopping from one character to another. Whatever we get wrong on the first pass, we can fix in revisions. And whatever we miss on the second draft, we can catch on the third pass. Or our editors or beta readers will catch it.

Even if a typo or a plot hole sneaks through, so what? Even if you are traditionally published and can do nothing to fix whatever mistakes get past you and your entire editorial team, it's not the end of the world. We're just telling stories. You'll tell a better one next time.

No matter where you are in your author's journey, whether you're still working on your first short story or your twentieth novel, open your mind to be a beginner. Be willing to take chances. Tackle new topics, new writing styles, new genres, new worlds and adventures for your characters. You are still a beginner. You are still learning. You will figure it out.

Reclaim the passion you had when you were first starting out, that joy and love of creating characters and putting them in situations, giving them goals and needs, raising the stakes, throwing obstacles in their path, and figuring out how to get them to where they need to go. Writing is fun. It can be a joyful experience. You know this because it was at the beginning. It can still be that way if you let it.

When you write yourself into a corner and you're not sure how to move the story forward, it's okay to pause and brainstorm your way out. Maybe you need to back up a bit and change the last chapter or two. Or maybe you will have to plant red herrings earlier in the story. Maybe you need to combine two characters or make some major change like switching from first person to a close third. It's okay.

Give yourself permission to do whatever you need to do. No fear. No shame. Remember, as it says in Frank Herbert's epic tome *Dune*, "Fear is the mind killer." And shame is the joy killer. Just be a beginner all over again with every new story. With every draft.

You can be excited about revisions. You really can. Sure, they seem like work. They may not feel as carefree as the rough draft. Your goals are a little different. You're trying to make the story better. But that can be fun too. You may have to use some affirmations to remind yourself to choose joy and love and passion while you're doing this. But you can. It works. And that positive energy will make the revision process so much more enjoyable.

The rules of writing don't have to be a burden. Remember, you are a beginner. You're not just learning how to write—you're a beginner on telling this particular story. Every story is unique.

Give yourself permission to try things and make

mistakes in how you're telling it, knowing you will fix those mistakes eventually. It is by taking these chances and pushing your skills that you get better at telling the next story.

Embrace the Beginner's Mind, and your author journey will be not only more successful but also more enjoyable.

12

Rediscovering the Joy of Creation

Years ago, I was editing a story, and I was miserable, mired deep in the Great Swampy Middle of the story. The plot was dull. The characters were boring. And I actually asked myself why I had to do this. And then I realized I didn't. Duh!

No one was making me write stories. Or even edit stories. I chose to do this. I wanted to do this. This was a labor of love, of joy. But somewhere along the way, I had lost that joy. What happened to it?

Part of the answer is that I discovered that writing was hard work. The adage "Find a job you enjoy doing, and you'll never work a day in your life" is a load of crap.

Writing engaging stories isn't easy. It can be a joy, and it can seem effortless when the words are flowing, but at other times, it's hard. It is work. It requires thought, intention, and effort. As Tom Hanks's character Jimmy Dugan said in *A League of Their Own*, "It's supposed to be hard. If it wasn't hard, everyone would do it. The hard is what makes it great."

So many people say, "One day, I'll write a novel" or

"One day, I'll write my memoir." But few people actually attempt this.

And of the few that attempt it, only a small percentage finish the rough draft. And of those who finish a rough draft, a tiny fraction of those get it published, either through a traditional publisher or by publishing it themselves.

And we all know why so few of those who talk about writing a book actually do it. Because it's freakin' hard. But it doesn't have to be miserable. Joy and work are not mutually exclusive.

If you've written a rough draft, that's awesome. That's something so few accomplish. Celebrate that! And if you've gone so far as to revise it, get it edited, and get it published, that's amazing. Truly!

And why are you doing it? I'm guessing that, at some level, you enjoy writing. You enjoy making stories and playing "what if." You enjoy creating characters and worlds (even if it's fictional versions of this world).

Or if you write nonfiction, you enjoy sharing your wisdom and knowledge. And if you write poetry, wow! You must really enjoy playing with words and creating wonderful imagery.

You love doing this. Even if sometimes, your muse takes an extended coffee break or goes on a long vacation without bothering to write. You love doing this, even when you've written yourself and your characters into a corner and struggle to figure out where to take the story next. Even if your sentences don't play nice with one another. Even when your soul bleeds after a critic or reader leaves a scathing one-star review.

It is so easy to lose touch with that feeling of love we have toward our process and our work. It's like a couple who, over the years, lose touch with that feeling of love for each other. The pressures of work and kids and finances and all of that can take a toll.

REDISCOVERING THE JOY OF CREATION

But guess what? You can bring back that loving feeling. You can fall back in love with your work. And that love can carry you through the difficult times. That love can be what makes or breaks a writer's career. Consider me a marriage counselor between you and your work.

Wherever you are with your current work in progress, I want you to focus on that now. Allow yourself to feel whatever feelings come up. Feelings of inadequacy, frustration, anger, fear, shame, whatever. Really let yourself feel those emotions. Own them. Maybe even say them aloud. "I feel upset." "I feel like a failure." "I feel like an imposter." "I'm frustrated with where this story is going." Whatever it is.

Okay, now take a deep breath, and when you exhale, imagine you're blowing out all of that negativity. Because none of it is really you. It's just thoughts about you. They don't define you. We've thought them. We've allowed ourselves to feel them, to acknowledge them. Now we can let them go. Blow them out. Like you're blowing out smoke or, at the very least, carbon dioxide. Every CO_2 molecule is taking away a bit of that negativity with it. Let that crap go. Don't need it anymore.

When you inhale, breathe in the love you have for writing, for creating, for playing "what if." Remember the passion you had way back when for writing and even for editing, for polishing your work into something special that would entertain, inform, or enlighten your readers. Remember that excitement of holding your first book. There is joy and love and passion there. You know it. Reclaim it.

Let yourself feel that passion, that love, that joy. Because you felt it then, and you can sure as heck feel it now. Breathe it in. Let that love attach itself to every oxygen molecule flowing through your windpipe. Feel that love filling your chest and spreading through your body, your heart, and your mind.

Exhale and let go of that negativity. Let go of the unreasonable expectations, the frustrations, the despair, and the shame. Keep doing this for five minutes, ten minutes, even thirty minutes. Try to do this at least once a day.

You can do this sitting at your keyboard, staring at your work in progress. Even if it's a blank screen or a blank sheet of paper. Or maybe a previous work. Allow yourself to feel whatever negative feelings come up when you look at it. Then blow them all away and breathe in that love you once felt for that project when it was just an idea. Let it transform your feeling for the project now. Let it fill your soul.

Because you chose to work on this project. You chose to be a writer. No one held a gun to your head and told you to do it. You were excited to work on this project at some point.

Don't let the "hard" get in your way of loving the project. It needs your love, your unique touch, your unique voice. It needs you. No one else can tell this story or explain this topic or share these thoughts the way you can. Your journey has brought you here. It has prepared you. Feel that love for this project again. And start writing.

Imagine what you can come up with when you do this before each writing or editing session. Let that love fill your heart and mind. Pour it out on the page.

If you find a typo in a finished work, don't beat yourself up. Your editors or beta readers (I hope you're using at least one of these) missed them too. If you're self-published, you can always fix it. If you're published traditionally, simply accept it and move on. It does no good to dwell.

Perfect is the enemy of great. A great painting can still have imperfections. A great novel can still have its flaws or perceived flaws. Look on Amazon for the books by your favorite author. They will have garnered their share of one-star reviews.

Look at movies starring your favorite actor or by your

favorite director. They've been in or directed at least one dog or two along the way. We're all human. We try things. Some work out better than we expected, while others turn out to be disappointments. And we move on.

I adore Lana and Lila Wachowski, and not just because they're transgender. Their movies *Bound* and *The Matrix*, as well as the mind-blowing series *Sense8*, are some of my favorites of all time. But *Jupiter Ascending*? Don't even get me started. Yeah, it has some interesting visuals, but it didn't move me the way their other work did.

But that's okay. Lana and Lila are not failures. They're not bad writers or directors. They are amazing, talented women. They push the envelope. They have created iconic works that have become part of our culture. Red or blue pill? They came up with that.

I'm not saying you will create such iconic works. But that doesn't give you permission to diss something just because you wrote it. If you can improve it, do so. But if it's finished and done, just learn to appreciate it. Your work isn't you. Its worth isn't your worth. It is merely a creative expression. Accept it for what it is and move on.

When rereading your published work, stop looking for the flaws. Look for the gems. Search for the turns of phrase that you are proud of. Look for those scenes that you put your blood, sweat, and tears into and savor them. Own the passion that went into them. Let yourself laugh at the funny bits and cry at the emotional, heartrending scenes.

There is a scene in *Iron Goddess* that still rips my heart out to this day when I read it. I cried when I wrote it. I cried when I revised it. It's not Shakespeare, but I still get a lump in my throat whenever I reread it. My eyes are watering right now thinking about it.

Iron Goddess isn't a bestseller. I haven't won any awards. I don't have an MFA. I'm just a recovering-alcoholic, suicide-surviving, transgender pansexual woman writing gritty crime thrillers about quirky queer women kicking ass. My writing isn't literary in the least. It's pulp fiction. My metaphors can be clichéd. My word choice even pedestrian.

But you know what? I love the stories I tell. I love the characters that I create. I love the issues that I explore. I love how accessible my writing is. You don't need a college degree to understand it. It is what it is.

Your writing is what it is. And with every new project, your skills will improve in ways you probably won't notice. But I bet your readers will. Mine do.

Love your writing where it is, as it is. Nourish it with love and passion, and it will grow. Your author voice will get big and strong. And when you get stuck in the Great Swampy Middle, when the editing gets tedious, reconnect with that passion and that love. Let it fill your heart and help you push through to the end.

13

The Comparison Delusion

Your voice, your projects will sound different from other authors. You're not Stephen King or Isabel Allende or Agatha Christie or Amy Tan or Lee Child or Toni Morrison or whatever bestselling author you idolize. You are you. And that is a good thing. Because your author voice is as valid as any other.

When you read your work, it will sound like you. Your experience will season every sentence you write, every character you craft, every plot you build.

You may tend to cringe when you become familiar with your author voice the way some people cringe when they hear an audio recording of their own voice.

"Oh, my goodness. Do I really sound like that?"

Yes! Yes, you do. And you should; it's you. And it's good.

You fell in love with writing. Maybe it's time to fall in love with your author voice. Read your work. If you're reading a rough draft, love it, knowing that you will be revising it and polishing it and making it better.

If you're reading a revised draft, love it for all the effort and love and passion you've put into it. Listen to what makes your unique voice special and valuable.

If you're reading one of your published works, love it for all the ways that you make telling this story or nonfiction book or poem special in a way no one else could.

There is a tendency to construe our not sounding like the authors we admire as some kind of flaw. We assume our uniqueness means that we suck. Our writing sucks.

What were we thinking with our dreams of grabbing hold of that brass ring? Silly childhood dreams. We read the bestsellers from our heroes then compare them to our pathetic stories. We are consumed with shame at the comparison. Such garbage. No wonder no one wants to publish or read our work.

Hello! Pity party for one!

Okay, sorry. Just kidding. We've all been there, my friend. Comparing our work with that of professional authors who've been writing books for decades is a common mistake. Never mind that we're just getting started in our career, still learning the craft. We so want to be like them, and yet it feels like we never will be. But that's okay.

The writing industry has changed tremendously over the years. When I was a kid in the late 1970s, the only legitimate way to get published was to look up publishers in *Writer's Market* and mail your query letter, first chapter, and a self-addressed stamped envelope and wait for weeks to hear back. In those days, you could even submit to the major publishers without an agent.

On the one hand, there were no personal computers to write on. We had typewriters (mine was a manual Smith Corona). If you made a mistake, you had to use a bottle of Wite-Out to fix the mistake and type over it. Or start all over on a clean sheet of paper. Maybe if you were lucky, you had a fancy typewriter that would white-over the mistake and let you correct it that way.

Fewer books were on the market then. Fewer people were getting published. Publishers invested in new authors, knowing their first few books probably wouldn't earn out advances. But with a little branding and marketing, the next one just might.

Back then, only self-indulgent, talentless hacks with money to burn and who couldn't get a publishing deal published their own work, which was why we called it vanity publishing.

E-books weren't a thing. Neither was Amazon. People bought books at brick-and-mortar stores like B. Dalton and Waldenbooks in the mall. I'm sure there were similar chains outside the US. There were also many more independent and used bookstores.

I point this out because what was true then, back when many of the "greats" made their bones, is not even possible today.

Publishers don't invest in authors the way they did in the twentieth century. They still give out huge advances but only if you're already a celebrity with a mega platform.

The hundreds of publishers that existed back then either went out of business or merged repeatedly until they became the Big Six, then the Big Five, and now the Big Four. Plus Amazon and a few small presses.

Pitching agents and publishers has changed dramatically. More agents opened up to online and email submissions (so long, SASEs!). Now, there are pitching events like PitMad on social media.

The change started the late 1990s when Amazon opened as an online book retailer running in the red for years. They were a disruptor, selling books for deep discounts. The old brick-and-mortar bookstores dismissed them as a passing trend until they found themselves struggling to compete. Many of them were forced to close their doors.

Amazon then made e-books commercially viable. A

huge new cadre of writers emerged who embraced this new technology, even as the old traditional publishers snubbed their noses at it, calling it a fad.

When I went shopping for an agent back in 2015, I submitted to ninety agents before I signed with an agency. And even then, we could get only an e-book-only deal with no advance. Very little marketing. After the first two books didn't meet their sales goals, they opted not to go for a third.

Meanwhile, self-publishing was becoming a legit path to authorship. Organizations like the Alliance of Independent Authors and indie authors like J. A. Konrath and Joanna Penn were showing the world what it looked like to be self-published while also producing professional-quality books.

Thus began the indie author gold rush. Hordes of writers, no longer constrained by the old gatekeepers, began throwing up their books online. Previously ignored voices began to be heard, reaching readers directly. New books began appearing by the millions, swamping the market.

Why am I telling you all this? Because comparing yourself to someone who became a household name back in the previous century simply doesn't make sense. Everything has changed. Your ability to write and edit a book has changed. Your ability to find a publisher or to become your own publisher has changed. And the number of books that readers can choose from has changed.

It would be like a high school ballplayer comparing themselves to Babe Ruth or Kareem Abdul Jabbar. It's simply not the same game.

Comparing your work to that of a seasoned veteran, especially if you only have a few books (or no books) under your belt, makes little sense. They've been at it a lot longer than you. They've had a lot more practice. When you've written as many words as they have, you will be much further along than you are.

THE COMPARISON DELUSION

But maybe you're not comparing yourself to the seasoned veterans. Maybe you're comparing yourself to your peers, authors who have roughly the same number of books to their name. And maybe they've won awards or have been able to quit their day jobs, while you're slogging out the words during your work breaks or in the wee hours of the morning or when the kids are down for their naps. And you wonder what you're doing wrong.

I can definitely relate to that. I've seen my peers win all kinds of awards and get major press coverage, while I'm struggling to pay for editors and cover designers.

We each have different author journeys with different backgrounds, experiences, amounts of available time, privilege, education, etc. All these factors play into the quality of our work.

The playing field is far from level. The influencers in the book world are filled with biases and always have been. While some are seeking out more diverse voices, many still give preferential treatment to white, cisgender, straight male authors who are traditionally published.

I found myself having to choose between writing stories about cis-het white guys if I wanted to be traditionally published or being true to myself and writing about trans and other queer women. I chose the latter, but it left me little option but to go the indie publishing route.

Last but not least, comparing your rough draft or first revision to someone else's finished work is nonsense. A rough draft isn't going to read like a professionally edited novel. I guarantee you Stephen King's rough drafts are rough. His publishing company still uses an editor for his work after he's gone through however many revisions on his own.

Of course, these logical reasons not to compare yourself to others probably don't change how you feel. Emotions aren't rational. Trying to use logic to silence that critical, self-deprecating voice pissing all over your work is futile.

Still, the time has come to dismantle the delusional impulse of comparing yourself to others. Time to expose the flaws in that absurd belief system. We have to go back to focusing on that Middle Way. We have to make a conscious choice to alter our thinking. We have to be willing to see what that nasty troll inside us is saying and replace it with a more loving, supportive voice.

Consider using these affirmations.

I am willing to let go of comparing myself to other writers.
I am willing to see the value of my own writing.
I am willing to celebrate the uniqueness that I bring to stories.
I am willing to love my unique voice.
I am willing to love my writing.
I am willing to accept compliments from readers.
I am willing to love the characters I create, to appreciate my word choices, to enjoy the plots, subplots, and sudden twists.

Feel free to modify the words to fit your situation or even add lines. The words aren't where the magic lies. It's in the intent. We are changing the direction of our thinking from negative to positive. Making this change isn't an overnight deal. It takes time. It's like trying to make a U-turn in an ocean liner. But we can do it.

When you feel comfortable with these affirmations, take out the words "am willing to" and give these mantras a little more juice.

I will no longer compare myself to other writers.
I see the value of my own writing.
I celebrate the uniqueness that I bring to stories.
I love my unique voice.
I love my writing.
I accept compliments from readers.

THE COMPARISON DELUSION

I love the characters I create, appreciate my word choices, enjoy the plots and subplots and sudden twists.

Wow! Those statements are bold. Our inner troll may scream and rant that we are delusional, that we're setting ourselves up for a big disappointment, that we're kidding ourselves, that we're nothing but a poser, an imposter. But that's just the old tapes playing. It's a manifestation of fear. And we don't have to live in fear anymore.

We're taking off the training wheels. We're declaring our independence from fear and insecurity and self-doubt. We don't need them anymore. They no longer serve.

We can instead embrace love. We can embrace that joy that first inspired us to write. It's still there, buried under all the fear and hard work.

We no longer need to feel like a second-rate Toni Morrison or James Patterson. We can choose instead to be the best version of ourselves, honoring everything that we bring to the page. All of our trauma and history and talent and education and challenges and choices. All of the stuff that makes us who we are today.

And as we do so, as we embrace being our best selves, we will gradually, even imperceptibly but continually, become even better versions of ourselves. Our fifth book will be much better than our first book. Our tenth book will be better than our fifth.

I wrote three books and countless short stories before I had one published. But that time and effort wasn't wasted. That was practice. That was an investment in myself. And it was worth it.

You are an awesome writer. Tell yourself that often. Remind yourself daily that you improve with every story or article or poem you write. You can be free of the delusion of comparing yourself to others.

14

Dealing with Feedback

If you are new to writing, I encourage you to get help from fellow writers. Join a local critique group that gets together every week or so to give one another feedback on what you've written. You can find a lot of them on Meetup.com. If a local critique group doesn't exist in your area, consider starting one or join one online.

Every critique group has their own guidelines. In most critique groups, you will share a chapter or a few pages. Don't show up with an entire novel and ask for feedback on the whole deal. Ain't gonna happen.

Some will require you to read it aloud. In other groups, your fellow writers will read your submission silently or ahead of time and then provide feedback.

Getting feedback from fellow writers, especially those who are at a similar stage of their author's journey, can be a wonderful way to learn the rules of writing while you develop a thick skin for constructive feedback. You're among peers who understand what it's like to learn the fundamentals of the craft. You're all in the same boat.

The first time you get a manuscript back from a critique

partner or from a professional editor, it can feel like someone just stomped on your heart and called your baby ugly. If it's a printed manuscript, all that red ink may resemble a crime scene photo. It can feel intimidating and leave you wondering if you should bother continuing.

The feedback is not proof that you failed. You didn't fail. No one is giving your story an F. They are pointing out where your writing can be improved. It is an opportunity to learn and grow and improve your story. Not a reason to shame yourself.

Granted, some writers don't know how to give proper feedback. Their critiques can be unduly harsh. They may say unhelpful things like "This story is garbage" or "This character is stupid." Ignore people like that. Seriously. They are only projecting their own insecurities onto your work.

Proper feedback shows you how you can improve your story or at the very least what isn't working. It should also let you know things you did well. There are always some redeeming qualities.

A typical critique might sound like, "I fell in love with this character, but the dialogue felt a little forced and info-dumpy. Don't open with the character waking up. You head-hopped from one character to another in this scene, but I like where the story is going."

Maybe a critique partner was pulled out of the story at one point, but they're not sure exactly how they would fix it. That's okay. It's not their job to fix everything for you, only to point you to the areas that need work. The knowledge that a certain point in the story wasn't working at least gives you a starting point for improvement.

You may also get conflicting feedback. I've had critiques in which a fellow writer loved one character and hated the other, while another writer had the opposite reaction. It can drive you crazy sometimes. Understand that every person reading your story will have their own opinion based on their unique experiences and reading preferences. Take what you like and leave the rest.

Getting feedback from beta readers can be even more frustrating. Beta readers are not necessarily writers. They don't always understand why an aspect of your story isn't working, only that they got bored. Look at where they got pulled out of the story and see how you, as a writer, can make it better.

When you receive feedback, take your ego out of the equation. It's not a personal attack on you. Your worth as a human being isn't being called into question.

At the same time, learn to trust your instincts. It's okay to ignore some feedback, especially if the person giving the critique doesn't normally read in your genre. I once gave a critique for someone who wrote British historical fiction. I saw the word "gaol" and thought it was a typo. It wasn't. What did I know? I write contemporary American crime thrillers. So in that instance, my feedback was not relevant.

You know best what kind of story you are trying to tell. Let your muse and inner editor analyze the feedback to help you tell the best story.

If you plan to publish, at some point, you will need a professional editor going through your work before publication. You many need several editors, starting with a developmental editor, a copy or line editor, and a proofreader. See, I told you this process was iterative.

If you are going the traditional publishing route, the publisher should cover the cost of these editors. That's one plus of going trad. If your publisher wants to charge you for the editing, that's a big red flag.

If you are going the indie (self-publishing) route, the editing cost will be on you. Hiring editors can get pricy—from a few hundred to a few thousand dollars, depending on what type of editors you are hiring and the length of your manuscript.

But trust me, a good editor is worth their weight in gold. They can take your story from good to great. And it's always better to learn what's wrong with your story from an editor than from a reviewer. I personally hire the fine folks at Red Adept Editing, but there is no shortage of qualified editors for hire.

A developmental editor addresses issues at the thousand-foot level. They focus on story structure, scene structure, and character development. If you are new to writing, a developmental editor is a must until you get a feel for structure and character. They will often give you an extensive report on the issues they discovered in your work.

Yes, a developmental editor is more expensive than other types of editors, but they help you solidify your storytelling.

A copy editor or a line editor focuses more on the flow of the writing, addressing sentence length, word usage, narrative voice, consistency of style, etc. There are subtle differences between a copy editor and a line editor, but all you really need to know is that they are both focused at a more granular level than the developmental editor. They are also generally less expensive per word than a developmental editor.

Last but not least, a proofreader targets all of those nasty typos—the misspelled words, the punctuation mistakes, and any remaining grammatical errors. This is the final polish. Trust me, you'd rather have your proofreader catch these mistakes than a reader or a critic. You don't want typos to bring down your reviews and ratings, even if you can fix them post-launch.

As with critique partners, you don't have to follow all the advice that your professional editors give you. It's okay to hold your ground on an issue if it tells the better story.

In my debut novel, *Iron Goddess*, I'd written a scene in which my main character, Shea Stevens, referred to a cop as Officer Commando because he was charging into her motorcycle shop, barking orders with guns drawn and no clue what was going on.

My editor suggested I change it to Officer Hero. I declined. I wanted the readers to understand Shea's low opinion of cops, considering she grew up in an outlaw biker family and later served time in prison herself. So I stuck with Officer Commando, not because it was my idea but because it told a better story. It more accurately revealed Shea's mindset.

When it comes to grammatical issues, especially commas and hyphens, I invariably accept whatever corrections my editors make. I have a decent understanding of these rules but nowhere near as good as my editorial team. On these matters, they are the experts, and I trust their judgment.

Keep in mind that even the best editors are human. They may miss some mistakes. My first two books went through myself, my agent, my developmental editor, my line editor, and my proofreader. All seasoned professionals. And yet some typos still sneaked through all of our expertise. It happens. Pobody's nerfect.

Getting good feedback from fellow writers or editors is crucial to the revision process. So what if your rough draft, or even your third revision, is full of typos, info dumps, POV shifts, tense shifts, and plot holes? Most early drafts are. It's the nature of the beast. That's what your critique partners, beta readers, and editors are for. Even the best writers need another set of professional eyes to take their manuscripts from good to great.

Feedback is not an indictment of your work or an indicator that you are not a talented writer or that the critiqued work is crap. It is a useful tool to help you improve your story. Welcome it. Embrace it.

15

The Delusion of Reviews

Reviews can make or break the success of a book. They are social proof and carry more weight than anything we, as authors, can say about our own books. The more reviews we get, the more social proof there is and the better the conversion rate between browsing readers and buyers.

That's a lot of pressure to deal with. When we get a glowing review, be it from an editorial reviewer at the *New York Times* or a reader on Amazon, it can send our emotions skyrocketing into the stratosphere.

But when we get a scathing review, it has as much, if not more, power to transform us into a whining, whimpering pile of goo. Suddenly, our inner troll is jumping up and down, saying, "See, I told you that story was crap! You're such a lousy writer."

How do we get off this emotional roller coaster when reviews are so critical to our success?

First, understand you have zero control over reviews once the book is out there. You control your writing, your editing, and your marketing process. What happens after it reaches a reader or reviewer is completely out of your hands.

If you're self-published, you can fix typos you find post-launch or modify the book description or BISAC categories in which the book is listed. But that doesn't change a review once someone has posted it. You have no control over reviews.

The good news is that you can get off this emotional roller coaster. You can take back the power that reviews have over you. The solution is simple. Stop reading the reviews of your books. No, really, just stop. They're not for you. They're for other readers.

There's a saying in Alcoholics Anonymous. What other people say about you is none of your business. This applies very much to book reviews. They are not your business. They were not written for you.

Besides, a few negative reviews are actually a good thing. A book with all five-star reviews looks suspect to the average reader. Especially if there are only a handful of reviews total. To potential buyers, it looks like the author asked his friends and family to give him glowing reviews, but no one else is reading the book.

If there are a lot of reviews, all five stars with nothing but praise, it appears as if someone hired a review farm to post fake reviews. Potential buyers see that and keep on scrolling. A mix of reviews is the strongest social proof.

Every bestselling book gets one- and two-star reviews and for a good reason. Not every book is for every reader. A book that is written with literary brilliance may get panned for being too hard to read or too boring and slow.

I personally tossed aside both Mary Shelley's *Frankenstein* and Bram Stoker's *Dracula* because they were so slow at building up to the exciting parts. And they are classics.

Books like J.R.R. Tolkien's *The Lord of the Rings* probably get one-star reviews because of how overly descriptive the narration is. Did he really have to describe every rock and crevice at Helm's Deep?

Romances get panned a lot for being formulaic. Thrillers and books in a more pulp fiction style get bad reviews for being unrealistic. Hard sci-fi, military fiction, and medical thrillers get scathing reviews for the slightest inaccuracy.

I've had a reader criticize a story because the time it took the main character to get from one location in Phoenix to another was, in their opinion, not accurate. The reviewer was wrong. I've traveled that route many times. But I can do nothing about the review that was posted.

And heaven forbid any typos escape your editing team's notice. I've been reading a thriller from one of the major traditional publishers and come across several typos. It happens. But reviewers will take issue when they come across them.

A book that is slotted into the wrong genre will get scathing reviews. A women's fiction novel without a happy-ever-after ending that is marketed as romance will get raked over the coals by devout romance readers. Some genres have very rigid tropes that must be met. Failure to do so will lead to bad reviews.

I have received complaints from reviewers that too many of my characters are LGBTQ, with accusations of me ramming my lifestyle down people's throats. Oh, dear. Not the gays!

I've received complaints about my books not having enough sex scenes. Or having too many sex scenes. Or too much profanity. Or the characters making stupid decisions.

There is nothing I can do about these. Zilch. I just accept that my books are not for every reader. Same is true of every book.

When I was a debut author, I read each review, looking for every nugget of wisdom to make my next story better. When I would come across a negative review, I would panic and contact my agent. "A reader said such and such about my book. Is this true? Should I be worried? Do I need to change something?"

Each time, she'd patiently respond, "No, that's just one reader's opinion. You're fine."

She was right. A review is just one reader's opinion. And as we often say, "Opinions are like assholes. Everybody's got one."

Even if the review is from a respected *New York Times* book reviewer or some other big-shot influencer, it's just one person's opinion. And guess what? We can't change it. It is what it is.

Some of you may be old enough to remember the days of Gene Siskel and Roger Ebert. If you don't know who they were, they were movie critics based in Chicago. They also had a popular show on PBS called *Sneak Previews*. Every week, they would give the latest films a thumbs up or down.

You know what I discovered? Many of the movies I loved the best were the ones that Siskel and Ebert hated. Same was true for many of the big-shot movie critics. They gushed about snooze fests like *The English Patient* but openly mocked the big summer blockbusters that audiences adored. My apologies to fans of *The English Patient*. Just wasn't my cup of Earl Grey.

This trend is still true today. My wife and I will scroll through Netflix or Prime Video and see a movie that we loved, but the Tomato-meter (critics) called it rotten. I loved the movie *Columbiana*, but critics despised it, giving it a 27 percent splat. I'm sorry, but Zoe Saldana kicking ass is always a winner in my book.

Maybe my wife and I have lousy taste in movies. Or maybe we simply have different tastes than the critics.

Just because some hotshot big-name critic doesn't like your book doesn't mean squat. They're one person with one opinion. They have biases.

My books don't get any editorial reviews. I don't even show up on their radar screen. But I don't care. I love what I write.

As authors, we obsess over the few bad reviews while ignoring the many glowing reviews. We can get a hundred reviews praising our book, but when one reviewer calls it trash, we question whether we deserve to call ourselves writers. Don't worry, you're not alone. We've all been there.

Most negative reviews are indicators that a particular reviewer is not your target market. If they post a review that says, "This book had too much violence and too much profanity," it will serve as a warning to others who don't like books with violence and profanity. And it will be a selling point to those who like that in books. It's a good thing.

How do we know which reviews are truly reflective of our work and which ones to ignore? The fact is that all of them are valid and none of them are. But as I said earlier, the best advice is simply not to read them. Ignore them. They weren't written for you.

If you absolutely must know what readers are saying about you, either grow the thick hide of a rhino or have someone you trust sort through the garbage to find the gems that you can use for marketing.

The only time you should be concerned about reviews is if a significant portion of reviews (more than 30 percent) garner only one or two stars. In that case, there may be a problem that needs to be addressed.

If there are a lot of complaints relating to genre tropes, maybe your book has been assigned to the wrong genre categories. Maybe your cover doesn't convey your book's true genre and is attracting readers with different expectations from what they're getting. If this is the case, do something about it if you can.

If you're traditionally published, talk to your agent or publisher. They may be willing to do something about it.

Or maybe not. If not, let it go and focus on your next book. You've learned a lesson about what not to do.

If you're self-published, see if there are other genres or subgenres that might be a better fit. Or see about getting a new cover that better conveys the genre your book fits into.

If your book is getting dinged for too many typos, talk to your editing team. See if they will take another pass at it. Again, if it's traditionally published, there may not be anything you can do. But if you're self-published, do everything you can to deal with the typos.

When you find reviews taking a toll on your peace of mind and your creative confidence, it's time to be like Elsa from *Frozen* and let them go. A great way to do this is with a meditation.

Get in your comfortable spot and close your eyes. Imagine all the negative reviews are a bundle of red helium-filled balloons (or purple balloons or black balloons). Really visualize these balloons as those reviews.

Now take one of them and release it. Watch it float away into the sky, getting higher and higher, smaller and smaller until it vanishes altogether. As it does, it's taking with it all the negativity associated with that review. Goodbye, review! See ya, but I don't need ya! Bye-bye! Away it floats until it's gone.

Don't grab that balloon again as it floats away. Let it go. You've acknowledged it. You've seen it. Now let it go bye-bye. Away in the breeze. So long, review.

If more reviews are eating at your soul, go through them one by one. See yourself releasing each one and freeing yourself of their hold on your psyche. Take a deep breath, then let go of all of that negativity when you exhale. Let it go. Goodbye. Gone, far away, never to return.

Don't go looking for the next negative review. Ignore your reviews from now on. Not your business. Not your drama. Not your circus, not your monkeys. You are under

THE DELUSION OF REVIEWS

no obligation to let them live rent-free in your head. Give them the heave-ho! They're outta here!

In large part, reviews are nothing but a distraction. They tell you little, if anything, about your work. They mostly indicate how well or poorly it fits with one particular reader. So don't get caught up in that delusion. Focus your energy instead on the joy of writing, the love of polishing a story, and the excitement of sharing it with the world.

16

The Delusion of Success

I will reiterate what I mentioned in the introduction. At the time of this writing, I have not earned six figures from my writing. I did earn five figures in revenue last year, but I spent a lot more on marketing and production. I haven't yet made a profit from my writing.

Meanwhile, I listen to writers on podcasts who are quitting their day jobs, paying off their mortgages, and absolutely killing it financially. I begin to wonder, what the hell am I doing wrong? I simply don't know.

I see some of my peers in crime fiction winning all kinds of awards. The Agatha, the Edgar, the Macavity, the Lambda, this award, and that award. I'm happy for them. I truly am. But my books never get nominated, much less win. It can be disappointing. *sigh*

I want to jump up and down and shout, "Hey! Over here! Look at my books! They're fantastic."

Maybe it's because I'm transgender. Maybe it's because my protagonists are queer women. Maybe it's because I walked away from traditional publishing and went indie. Or maybe the winners are just that much better than me.

Or maybe it's just dumb luck. Maybe my turn will come. Maybe, maybe, maybe.

Have you ever felt like that? Wondering why your books aren't selling more? Wondering why no one nominates them for an award? Wondering if you should even bother writing more?

What do you do when your fellow writers are winning awards, earning huge advances, and quitting their jobs to write full-time, while you're sitting here in the corner with your backlist of books all but ignored by everyone?

Here's what I do. I sigh, eat a pint of Ben & Jerry's, and remember something that so easily gets forgotten in all the sparkly trappings of success.

I remind myself that I love writing. I love telling stories. I love making up characters and plots and twists. And I love sharing them with the world. I love hearing from my fans.

I don't do it for the fame or fortune or awards. I do all of this because I love doing it. This is why I bother writing the next story.

Here's another thing we forget. Not everything is rosy for those to whom success appears to have come so easily.

I have a friend who releases a ton of books every year and makes a lot of money doing it. She writes full-time, gets a lot of great press, and lives in a beautiful house. She's living the dream. Right?

But you know what? She's also struggling financially. Yes, she's selling a lot of books, but she also spends a lot of money on ads and related expenses. She has a lot of personal expenses, too—raising a family, keeping up the house, dealing with life. And the pandemic made things hard on her, just as it did for the rest of us.

I've heard about successful full-time authors forced to go back and get a day job again. That's hard because some have been out of their previous professions long enough that getting back in is nearly impossible.

THE DELUSION OF SUCCESS

I used to be a programmer. Then I took a few years off to take care of my in-laws. When they both passed a few years later, I went looking to get hired again as a programmer.

But I was a middle-aged, transgender woman who had been out of the industry for several years. The world of programming had changed. I was obsolete. No one would hire me. I ended up taking a low-wage job to make ends meet and have health insurance.

Success is a delusion. You can be flush one day and broke the next. You can't depend on success as proof that you are a good writer. Your author journey will always have ups and downs.

In the traditional publishing world, you can get dumped by your publisher or your agent and suddenly find yourself back at square one. Your editor could quit. Your publisher could go out of business. And again, you're back at square one, while the books they published are lost in limbo. I've seen it happen to many of my fellows. It's heartbreaking.

In the self-publishing world, you can suddenly get banned from publishing on Amazon for no reason (it has happened to people I know) or from advertising on Facebook (which can be crucial to selling books across retailers). Big, unexpected changes happen all the time.

If you sell books on Kindle Select (which puts books in Kindle Unlimited), Amazon could change their revenue calculation algorithms. Suddenly, you're making a fraction of what you were. It has happened before and will happen again. Count on it.

There are no guarantees of success. Any success you find may be fleeting. Change is constant.

I know all of this can be depressing, but my point is that the one thing you can count on is the love for your own work and your enjoyment of the process.

I know, I know. Life would be better if we had all of those trappings of success—the awards, the bestseller status, the six-figure advances or annual revenue. If only we could quit our dreary day job and write full-time. I get it.

But provided that your basic needs are being met as you are, then let me assure you that those markers of success won't guarantee your happiness if you aren't happy now.

There is a mindset that I call the misery conspiracy. No, I'm not suggesting someone's out to get you and make you sad. Rather, you yourself are conspiring to keep yourself miserable.

Here's how the misery conspiracy works. No matter where we are or what's going on in our lives, we keep telling ourselves we'll be happy when…

I'll be happy when I finish writing this rough draft and can go on to editing. I'll be happy when I'm done with these revisions and can send it off to a publisher. I'll be happy when I find a publisher. I'll be happy when I can call myself a bestseller. I'll be happy when I get a review in the *New York Times*. I'll be happy when one of my books wins an award. I'll be happy when I make a profit from my writing. I'll be happy when I can quit my day job. I'll be happy when I get interviewed on *Fresh Air*. I'll be happy when…

At first glance, these statements look perfectly reasonable. But they are nothing but ways in which we sabotage our happiness. We'll always come up with excuses for why we can't be happy now. And this is a choice. We are choosing to be miserable now, no matter what we have, no matter what we've achieved, no matter how good our lives are. We keep postponing our happiness.

If we can't derive any happiness from the act of writing, then the awards and revenue and recognition won't mean anything. They will be like cotton candy, dissolving in our mouths. None of them are guaranteed anyway, even if we work really hard. So why deprive ourselves of happiness waiting for these things?

This is why making gratitude lists is so powerful. It counteracts the misery conspiracy by focusing on what we are happy about now.

I am grateful to be able to write this story.
I'm grateful to be a member of a critique group that is helping me learn the craft.
I'm grateful to have found a form of artistic expression that gives me joy.
I'm grateful to have created an outline for this story.
I'm grateful to be using my knowledge and creativity to revise this story.
I'm grateful to live in a world where I can reach out to agents and publishers online instead of waiting to get a letter in the mail.
I'm grateful to live at a time where I can publish my own work.
I'm grateful for all the amazing writers I've connected with around the world.

Maybe you will go on to get a six-figure publishing deal. Maybe your next book will win an award. Maybe you will get interviewed by Stephen Colbert.

But whether any of those happen or not, you can choose to be happy now, cherishing the process of writing, editing, building an author brand, connecting with readers, etc. You can be happy exactly where you are on your current project. You simply have to choose to be.

Consider all the creative professionals who achieved amazing success as actors, musicians, or artists of any kind, only to lose themselves in depression and substance abuse. They get so caught up in holding on to that initial thrill of success and pushing to reach the next level, telling themselves they'll be happy when… but no matter how many goals they achieve, the one thing they fail to achieve is actual happiness. There will always be something else they *must* achieve before they will let themselves be happy.

Having goals is good. Having achievable goals is excellent. I will write a thousand words a day and complete this next book by such-and-such a date. I will reach out to a dozen podcasts and explain why I would be a good interviewee for their show. I will rework my book blurbs to make them more engaging. I will learn how to make my Facebook ads profitable. I will send out a newsletter and share a new short story or an anecdote with my subscribers.

These goals are all achievable. They are within your control. We can find joy in each of these activities, some more than others.

But we have no control over whether we win awards or make a bestseller list. There are things we can do to improve our chances, such as writing excellent books that are professionally edited with professionally designed covers and exciting blurbs. We can learn how to create engaging newsletters that subscribers look forward to opening (I strongly suggest reading Tammi Labrecque's excellent book *Newsletter Ninja* for that).

We can search out podcasts that interview authors like us, familiarize ourselves with their formats, and contact them. We can take a course or read a book about running ads and learn how to make them profitable. But that's it. The rest is a crapshoot.

We must keep our focus on the here and now. Be present. Find joy in this moment, right where you are, doing whatever activity you are doing right now, whether it's writing, editing, analyzing ads, learning how to improve your skills, whatever. Find your joy now.

Finding your joy doesn't mean you won't get frustrated from time to time. When the words won't flow. When every ad you run seems to flop. When the sales numbers aren't what you hoped they'd be. When your subscribers

THE DELUSION OF SUCCESS

don't open your emails or click the links. But don't get stuck there.

Re-center yourself. Take a deep breath. Use the meditations and affirmations in this book. Make a gratitude list every morning. Be willing to see things differently. Be willing to see each activity differently. Be willing to find joy in each activity. Because the trappings of success may or may not come. But your happiness is in the here and now, not in the delusions of success.

17

Shiny Object Syndrome

If you've been a writer for any length of time, you're probably familiar with shiny object syndrome. If not, imagine you're a third of the way through your work in progress, deep in the Great Swampy Middle. You've introduced your main characters. You've hit the inciting incident. And now your heroes are going through a series of try-fail cycles to reach their goal.

Aaaand you're bored senseless.

Maybe you're not sure exactly where the story is going. Or maybe the dialogue feels forced and trivial. The scenes aren't exciting. Your team of heroes is licking their wounds from their last failure and making plans, but nothing is actually happening.

And then you get a spark of inspiration. Not for this story. No, no, no! This is a brilliant idea for a different story. This idea grips your soul. You're excited about it. Maybe it's an idea for a cool character. Or a fascinating twist to a story. Or a new world that you could spend months developing. A research topic that you could plunge down the rabbit hole and explore. There's so much energy around this exciting new idea.

That, my friend, is the shiny object. It happens to us all. Our muse is drowsing along in our current project and then sees this shiny object and absolutely must pursue it like a cat after a laser dot.

It's okay if this happens. Really. It's not the end of the world. It's okay if it happens with some frequency.

But if you catch yourself abandoning project after project to go chasing after shiny new objects, you'll finish nothing. And that can be okay too. If your goal isn't to publish but just write story beginnings and jump around from idea to idea, go for it. I have friends who like to do this. It's totally cool.

However, if you want to publish your work and find yourself not finishing projects, then it's time to address the situation.

The problem isn't the shiny new object. Coming up with a new idea for a story is awesome. The problem isn't how excited you are about it. All of that is good. You should be excited about your story ideas.

It's okay to chase after a shiny object once in a while. It only becomes a problem when you don't finish anything while still planning to publish. Because that's kind of a rule in publishing. You have to finish a story before you publish it. Crazy, right?

If you keep abandoning projects to chase after shiny objects, then every shiny new project will, in turn, become the next project you abandon.

In a way, it's kind of like a road trip. You're so excited as you pack the suitcase and load the car then stop at the convenience store to fill up the gas tank and buy lots of unhealthy snacks. Woo-hoo! Road trip! So exciting! Visions of all the wonderful things you will do and see fill your mind.

Then a hundred miles out of town, that long ribbon of

asphalt seems to stretch on forever. The scenery starts to all look the same (especially if you live in the desert like I do). The songs on the radio lull you to sleep. Are we there yet? Are we there yet? Are we there yet?

Our enthusiasm for our writing project often wanes when the writing begins to feel like work. We've already gone through the exciting part of creating the world and the characters. Now we have to knuckle down and figure out a plot structure that will sustain the reader's interest. Right now, it's barely sustaining our interest. If we're bored, the reader will be too.

What do we do when that shiny new object pops up in our head, luring us away from our current project like a siren's song?

Here's what I do. I write the gist of this shiny new idea somewhere. A lot of us have a "story ideas" document or folder. Put the ideas for the shiny object story idea there so that you can come back to it later.

Here's what I don't do. I do not go on a major brainstorming jag. Just record the essentials you already have and save it for later.

Once you've written the idea for the shiny new object, get back to your current project, the one on which the glitter has faded. I know, writing that story feels like a slog. Your goal now is to reclaim the excitement and energy you had when you started it. Because at one point, you couldn't wait to write this story.

How does Stella get her groove back? How do you reclaim your passion for the work in progress? Remind yourself why you love writing.

Is it just the beginning you get excited about? Or can you find joy in the middle? Can you learn to love brainstorming these try-fail cycles? Can you push through and relish the challenge of trying to wrap up the story threads into an exciting conclusion? I bet you can.

One thing I do when I lose the initial excitement or get stuck somewhere in the plot is find a comfortable place to stretch out (I'm fond of my recliner, but anywhere you like to relax will do), put on some nature sounds (falling rain is very good for this), and let my mind drift into a semi-conscious state. I'm not asleep, not fully awake either. I just shove my logical brain out of the way so I can take advantage of my creative subconscious. It's sort of like lucid dreaming.

And then I picture wherever I am in the story. I look at the characters. What are they trying to accomplish, both big goals and immediate goals? What is standing in their way? What else might stand in their way? What if they fail? What else might they try? How might the stakes get higher and the danger increase?

Now, I write crime fiction, so you might have a different approach. If you write romance, maybe you're looking at your two main characters. How do they meet? How do they initially feel toward each other? What's keeping them apart? What might they try to get past that? What circumstances might arise that would throw them together? Or force them further apart?

Throw out ideas and play with them no matter how crazy they seem. No matter how many times the same idea has already been used by you or other writers. You're not writing anything down. You're just playing pretend. You're spitballing. Allow for illogical ideas. Because sometimes, the illogical ideas lead to unexpected ideas that work. This is a free-flow state. Let it be fun. Enjoy experimenting with these characters and plot ideas. What unexpected things from their past might arise?

You know that energy that comes from world-building a new story or coming up with a new character or a plot idea. Tap into that but with your current story. You can do it. Fall back in love with these characters. Play with them like dolls or action figures but in your mind. Make play fun again.

I do this throughout the rough draft process sometimes. Sometimes I do it when I discover a horrible plot hole and get stuck in the revision process.

Why didn't Jinx just go grab her fugitive? What was keeping her from him? Was it a result of something she did previously that came back to bite her? What elements from earlier in the story can I pull in? Did her fugitive have help? Where might he actually be hiding?

If that doesn't work, try freewriting. Write a crappy version of the scene and then go over it again and write a less crappy version. Keep doing affirmations such as:

I love the characters in this story.
I love writing this story.
I love coming up with conflicts and resolutions and increasing the stakes.
I love brainstorming new ideas and new plot twists and new scenes.

You get the idea. Use all the tools I have shared to reclaim that creative energy and passion for writing.

These techniques may take a while to work. You may lay down and do some semi-conscious brainstorming for ten minutes or even an hour and still not come up with any new ideas. Try it again later.

Try writing in a different location or listen to different music or background noise. Try writing at a different time of day.

Keep the story problem in the back of your mind throughout your day. When you're waiting in line at the store, staring at those awful tabloid magazines. Listening to podcasts. Reading books by other people. Listening to the news. You know by now that inspiration comes from all kinds of sources. You have to fill the well before you can draw from it.

There are some things you should not do. Don't shame yourself for getting shiny object syndrome. Don't shame yourself for not coming up with exciting new ideas right away, no matter how many times you try these techniques to re-energize your writing and get the ideas flowing.

Don't berate yourself as a writer. Don't hate your characters or what you've written so far. If it's a rough draft, let it be a rough draft. If it's a revised version with typos and plot holes, accept it as such. It's a work in progress. No big deal.

Be gentle with yourself, your work, and your process. Embrace the joy and uncertainty of creativity. This isn't a science. It's a craft. It's a process. And as I stated early on in this book, it is messy. You try various things. Sometimes they work. Sometimes you have to try them in different ways or multiple times before they work. And sometimes you have to try a fresh approach entirely. But keep at it with patience and gentleness.

The shiny object will still be there once this project is finished and off to the editor.

18

Writer's Block

Writer's block. Those two words can strike terror in writers of all levels. Staring at the blank screen or paper but nothing is coming to mind. Our muse has ghosted us with no forwarding address.

Marketing guru Seth Godin states in several of his books, "Writer's block is a myth. You never hear about a plumber getting plumber's block. Writer's block is nothing more than fear."

He's right, of course. Fear and creative self-doubt are a big part of writer's block. You are so afraid of making mistakes and not living up to previous projects that your brain goes blank. The inner troll immediately dismisses any ideas you come up with as garbage.

Letting your creative well run dry can contribute to writer's block. That happens when you become so focused on writing that you run out of ideas.

Burnout can also be a contributing factor. You've pushed yourself so hard for so long, struggling to meet deadlines, that your muse has collapsed into a trembling heap, and your mind and body have nothing left to give.

Let's explore each of these elements, starting with fear.

I struggle with this sometimes after I complete one project and begin a new one, even if I already have a rough idea of what the new story will be about. Switching gears from finishing energy (focusing on making everything perfect prior to publication) and marketing/launch energy (when I'm trying to reach as many people as I can on release day) to creative/drafting energy can be tough.

We can tend to want to make the first page, the first paragraph, and the first line perfect right out of the gate. No info dumps. No boring dialogue. Just full-on excitement and literary brilliance that immediately draws the reader in.

Only we know that writing doesn't work that way. Creation is an iterative process. Creation is messy.

It can take a conscious effort to say, "No, inner editor. Time for you to be quiet and let the muse play. Time to just put words on screen and allow them to be clunky and rough. This is the drafting stage."

Even after eight novels, I have to consciously shift gears and tell myself this. I have to put the editor back in the closet and let my muse play. I have to give myself permission once again to write something rough and unpolished with typos, plot holes, awkward dialogue, and info dumps.

If you don't know what you want to write next, just play a little. Start with a character and describe them. Not so much hair color or body type but what makes them interesting and quirky. What's their driving principle (e.g., honesty, loyalty, survival, self-sacrifice)? Imagine a situation in which they would do the opposite but for a logical reason.

Experiment with worlds or situations or conflicts. Just play and allow yourself to enjoy playing. The ideas will come. First the lousy ideas, then mediocre ideas, then the better ideas, and eventually the knock-your-socks-off ideas. Trust your process.

Maybe you're afraid you just don't have the skill set

to write the story you want to write. For example, you want to write a historical novel, but you're afraid of using anachronistic language. Or you want to write a murder mystery but aren't sure about proper police procedures versus the bogus portrayal on many TV shows.

If creative self-doubt is the case, then use the tools I've shared earlier in the book—meditation, affirmations, journaling, connecting with other authors and getting real, being willing to see your writer self and your writing differently, etc.

Freewriting is an especially good tool to at least get something down on the page, even if it's "I don't know what to write. I don't know what to write. I'm afraid of trying an idea and failing."

When your inner critic warns you that something you want to write is a mistake or that you don't have the chops, reply, "So what?" Be willing to make mistakes. Embrace the imperfection.

Kathy Reichs has written more than a dozen books about Dr. Temperance Brennan, a forensic anthropologist who goes out into the field and solves murders and catches bad guys, even though real forensic anthropologists don't do that. It's okay. In Reich's fictional world of Dr. Brennan, they do. It's okay. Her massive fanbase doesn't care.

If there is a story you want to write but you lack basic background information, research whatever you're uncertain about.

Connect with other authors in your genre. One of the amazing things about social media is that we can connect with all kinds of people all over the world.

You can also find books, documentaries, YouTube channels, Facebook groups, and Pinterest pages on every subject imaginable.

I'm a member of Facebook groups that are geared toward writers who need help learning about police procedures, legal situations, or medical trauma. I'm sure there are groups for historical fiction authors needing help with language or about customs or clothing or whatever.

One time I needed to describe what a modern-day fifteen-year-old boy's room looked like. I had no idea, since I didn't have kids. So I asked my friends online. I did a Pinterest search. I got a lot of great ideas.

Currently, I'm working on a story in which my main character has to rescue someone from a cult. So I watched a bunch of documentaries on various cults. I read books by parents trying to rescue their adult children from cults. I learned a lot.

Research can be fun. Sometimes too much fun. It's easy to get lost down the rabbit hole. Sometimes we use it as an excuse not to write. You get to decide when you've reached that point. Be kind with yourself if you find you're putting writing off.

One of the side benefits of doing research is that it sparks ideas. Keep a journal of those ideas when they come up. Maybe you'll use them. Maybe you won't. Maybe they will generate even more ideas.

If you're struggling with a particular aspect of the writing craft, whether it's dialogue or description or story structure or whatever, there are tons of books out that will teach you how to master these skills. Ask your fellow writers for suggestions if you're unsure. Most authors love to help one another.

Take time away from writing if you need to. Let the creative well fill back up. Be gentle with yourself. Be okay with making mistakes. Love your muse and editor, while learning to ignore your inner troll.

If you feel overwhelmed by the whole pressure to publish, worried that what you're working on will never be good enough to publish, then work on something that you have no intention of publishing. It is perfectly valid to write something that will not be published.

I often joke that when my muse doesn't show up when I want to write, I just write garbage until she finally pops her head in and says, "Here, let me show you how to do it."

Our muse is us. Our muse is our creative self. And sometimes, if we've been overly harsh or get so caught up with making things perfect, our muse doesn't even want to show their face. They don't want to hear all that negativity from our self-doubt. But we can lure our muse back by simply writing anything without judgment. We can create a safe space for our muse to create and express without fear.

19

When the Creative Well Runs Dry

If the ideas are simply not coming, maybe your creative well has run dry. You do not know what you want to write about. No idea for a main character, much less a setting or plot. You're just blank, empty.

I remember experiencing this for a bit after my publisher decided not to extend my outlaw biker series after the first two books. I had plenty of ideas for more books in the series, but for the time being, that series was done. Kaput. No other publisher would pick up the series when the first two books didn't meet my first publisher's expectations. It left me starting from scratch, and I had no ideas.

When the creative well runs dry, what do we do? We fill the well. We read novels. We watch television and movies. We read news stories. We spend time with friends and family. There is no telling where a spark of an idea may come from.

We may tend to think that in filling our creative well, we will be tempted to steal someone else's ideas. It's why some authors refuse to read in their genre while they are in drafting mode. I get this. But you need not worry. There is nothing new under the sun. There is no revolution. Only evolution. You can take an idea from multiple sources, combine them, and add your own twist.

How many stories about vampires are there? Millions. Each one has its own take on the mythos, starting with Bram Stoker's *Dracula*. That character alone has been reinvented countless times.

Look on your favorite online book retailer, and you will find books about vampires who are vulnerable to garlic or crosses, vampires who can only be killed with sunlight or silver, vampires who are sparkly, vampires who are ravenous monsters, vampires who are sexy, and vampires who drink only animal blood or artificial blood.

Don't worry about being influenced. Just be willing to take whatever ideas you borrow/steal in a whole new direction.

When I was struggling to come up with an idea for a new series, I talked to my wife about it. I explained that I didn't want to write a police procedural or an amateur sleuth cozy mystery. I wanted something gritty and action-packed. She suggested writing about a bounty hunter.

I let the idea percolate. I had read several of Janet Evanovich's Stephanie Plum novels. If you're not familiar with the series, Stephanie Plum is a bounty hunter in New Jersey. She kind of bumbles her way through solving cases with help from her oddball associates. She is very hard on vehicles. The series is fun, humorous, and lighthearted, nothing like my writing style.

But I could take that concept and make it my own. I could write a gritty action thriller series about a bounty hunter in Arizona. One who was transgender like me. One who was into comic books and cosplay.

Now that I had an idea for a character, I needed to learn how bounty hunters in Arizona operated. I watched countless YouTube videos on channels by professional bounty hunters. I read books and articles about bounty hunters and their work. I interviewed bounty hunters.

All of this research wasn't just to learn how bounty hunters operated. I was filling the well. As I learned about real cases, my brain began to go into "what if" mode. What if my bounty hunter character was pursuing a fugitive like this? Where would a fugitive like this hide? How would my bounty hunter track them down? What kind of try-fail cycles could I use?

And then I stumbled across a story in *Rolling Stone* magazine about a young woman who murdered her mother after years of abuse.

For much of her life, Gypsy Rose Blanchard believed she suffered from multiple debilitating childhood diseases that left her wheelchair-bound, bald, and requiring constant medical attention.

Only it turned out that Gypsy wasn't sick at all. She was abused. Her mother, Dee Dee Blanchard, had Munchausen by proxy, a psychological condition that led her to make her child appear sick to gain sympathy and attention. She forced her daughter to endure countless medical tests and bilked charitable organizations for untold donations. It went on for nearly twenty years.

As a teenager, Gypsy realized this was all a horrible hoax. She began to sneak onto the internet and developed an online romance with a young man who had a criminal history. In her isolation-induced naivete, she considered him her boyfriend.

Desperate to be free of her mother's abuse, Gypsy and her "boyfriend" murdered Dee Dee then disappeared. After police discovered Dee Dee's body, they initially assumed Gypsy had been kidnapped. A massive search was conducted to find and rescue her.

When Gypsy was found alive and unharmed in a motel room, she was arrested. The trial made national news.

Eventually, she pleaded guilty to second-degree murder and was sentenced to ten years in prison.

The tale is tragic. As a survivor of emotional abuse, I was moved. But I was also inspired.

What if someone like Gypsy Blanchard disappeared shortly before her court date? Was she kidnapped? Was she really a cold-blooded murderer? What if there was more to the story? What if my bounty hunter, Jinx Ballou, was assigned to return her to custody?

Although there are some seeds of similarity between my first Jinx Ballou novel, *Chaser*, and the Blanchard tragedy, I took the story in very different directions. I won't detail how (because I don't want to spoil anything), but if you were to compare the Blanchard case to *Chaser*, you would see major differences. I took the seed of an idea from real life and then turned it upside down it to tell a compelling crime thriller.

Read heavily in the genre you write. But also read in other genres. Sometimes a nugget of inspiration from a completely different kind of story can be combined with the tropes of your genre to create something that hits all the right beats but is also fresh and new.

I don't write romance or sci-fi or fantasy, but I do read books in those genres. It has helped me come up with ideas for subplots and even overarching plots that span multiple books.

A few years ago, I read a unique crime thriller about a serial killer by my friend Isabella Maldonado. There are a gazillion serial killer stories. Some say there are too many. But Isabella took it in a new direction by tying in the viral social media phenomenon as a key part of the plot.

The result, *The Cipher*, wasn't just another serial killer crime thriller. It was an exciting, engaging, page-turning commentary on how we engaged with social media.

That book later inspired me to explore how people

weaponized deepfake videos and other cutting-edge technology to attack vulnerable people and to sway public opinion. And I did it while telling a balls-to-the-wall action thriller.

If you find your creative well is running dry, fill it up with all kinds of stuff until the ideas once again percolate. Then play with them until they start to form the seeds of a story.

20

Dealing with Burnout

Sometimes the ideas refuse to come because we've pushed ourselves too hard for too long. Our minds and bodies are exhausted. We hit the wall.

The best definition I've found for burnout comes from helpguide.org. It states, "Burnout is a state of emotional, physical, and mental exhaustion caused by excessive and prolonged stress. It occurs when you feel overwhelmed, emotionally drained, and unable to meet constant demands."

Burnout can be caused by any number of factors, including our day jobs, family responsibilities, financial issues, health issues, and even our author careers. When any of these put us in a prolonged crisis mode, it can quickly lead to burnout.

With burnout, we may or may not have ideas for stories. If we do, we don't feel like writing. Burnout is common with authors on a rapid release track for an extended period. You push, push, push to get out the words, meet deadlines, launch titles, and start the next one, repeating the cycle over and over again until you completely lose the joy of writing.

Burnout can also happen to authors who put out only

one or two books a year, especially when other aspects of their lives become stressful.

If you find yourself exhausted (mentally and/or physically) most of the time, hating activities you used to enjoy (such as writing), unable to produce professional work (cutting corners), and arguing with loved ones more frequently, and your mindset is becoming increasingly pessimistic and negative, then you are in the midst of a burnout or well on your way there.

Burnout can affect not only your writing but can also threaten your life. It can lead to serious mental health problems, including depression, anxiety disorders, panic attacks, substance abuse, and suicidal ideation, as well as physical health issues like chronic headaches, gastrointestinal disorders, heart attacks, strokes, etc.

If we're struggling to meet editorial deadlines or financial goals, it can be tempting to ignore the symptoms of burnout until our whole mind and body shut down and we end up in the hospital.

Burnout makes our creative self-doubt infinitely worse. It's like our inner troll is running the show and turning into a tyrant, attacking everything in our life, including people we love.

What do we do when we find ourselves on this dark road of burnout? We have to stop. We have to rest. We have to recharge and heal. No excuses.

We may have to put off our deadlines for a few months or years. I know, editors hate it when you miss a deadline. And readers who are champing at the bit for your next book will complain.

But most people, including editors, publishers, agents, and fans, would rather you take care of yourself and postpone a deadline than put yourself in the hospital or worse, end up in the morgue.

If you broke your wrist and could not write for an

extended time, people would understand. Your agent and editor and publisher and fans would all wish you a speedy recovery. They might not be happy about the wait, but they wouldn't hold it against you.

Recovery from burnout is no different. No one wants you suffering for your craft. There is nothing noble about burning out. Trying to push through it usually results in poorer output anyway.

You may need to get professional help. That means talking with your physician or psychiatrist about medication for anxiety, depression, or other issues. And there is no shame in this.

Over the past few months, I've been hit with a lot of financial stressors. Seems like every time I turn around, something else is breaking and needs fixing. And it always seems to cost several hundred or several thousand dollars I don't have.

I began having panic attacks and insomnia. Even using my recovery tools wasn't enough. My ability to write was fine, so it wasn't creative self-doubt. But anytime I thought about something else in the house or car breaking, my chest would tighten and my pulse would race as if I were having a serious cardiac event.

I contacted my physician, who prescribed me something to help my anxiety. It's helping me function while I dig myself out of this financial situation. If I hadn't done this, the anxiety could very well have begun to affect my writing as well.

No one likes asking for help. No one likes missing deadlines. No one likes having to stop doing something that at one time brought us joy. No one likes having to put the brakes on everything and recover. But sometimes, that is the only thing we can do. Sometimes, it is the most loving thing we can do for ourselves and our readers.

Burnout isn't a failure. Burnout doesn't have to be the

end of a writing career, unless we ignore it until it's too late. Burnout is a serious situation but one that we can bounce back from.

Burnout is an opportunity we can learn from. We can learn more about who we are as human beings and as authors. We can learn more about our creative process. We can learn how better to take care of ourselves so that we don't end up back here anytime soon.

Recovering from burnout may mean we have to reassess how many books we write and publish in a given amount of time. We may have to change how we connect with our fanbase and market our author brand. We can use these lessons to create new characters. Stephen King did it, as have many other authors who've struggled with burnout.

Obviously, it's better not to burn out. But if we do, and if we recognize the signs and take care of ourselves, we can rebound as even better authors.

21

Pay Attention to Self-Talk and Feelings

As writers, it is important to pay attention to how we talk to ourselves. Even if we don't voice them aloud, we constantly have conversations with ourselves in our heads. Going over our to-do list for the day. Expressing our frustration when something doesn't work out as planned. Guiding our way through a complicated task.

Self-talk is very revealing. How do you talk to yourself? With respect, kindness, and encouragement? Or with criticism, cynicism, and shame? All too often, self-talk is negative.

Dammit, why did I do that? I'm so stupid. Why can't I remember her name? I'm such an idiot. Geez, how many times do I have to do this till I get it right?

The words we use toward ourselves now reflect language that adults used toward us when we were young. I heard a lot of criticism from my mother when I was growing up, disparaging me, discouraging me, controlling me.

> *Why can't you do better? You'll never make a living doing that. That's too hard for you. Don't bother. You're changing sex to become a woman? After all that I've done for you, how could you do this to me? You're an abomination. You'll be an ugly woman. No one will love you.*

When I became an adult, I echoed that language toward myself. I became drawn to other people (such as my abusive ex-husband) who echoed that language toward me. And because I had normalized it internally, I took it for far too long. I spent a lot of time in therapy and in support groups before I could let go of that negative self-talk.

In recovery, we called it "the old tapes." It's as if we made recordings of the shaming talk we heard as children, and now we repeatedly replay them in our minds, the words coming out of our own mouths.

Sometimes, our creative self-doubt is a form of those "old tapes."

> *You're no good at that.*
> *That story is pathetic.*
> *No one would want to read that, much less pay to read that.*
> *No publisher will want to sign you.*
> *You'll never find an agent.*
> *You don't deserve that award you won.*
> *You have no talent for writing.*
> *You're a fraud.*

To counter this negative self-talk, we must first acknowledge it. We must listen to what these negative messages are telling us. We can't simply ignore them. You can't defuse a bomb unless you know how it's wired. Those thoughts have formed strong pathways in our brains from years or decades of hearing them from others and ourselves.

To get a good look at what we tell ourselves, we should write them down, recognizing as we do that these negative messages may not be true. They are just the old tapes playing. But we are paying attention, letting this broken, wounded part of ourselves spew for a moment.

And once that negative part of ourselves, our inner troll, has said their piece, we can begin changing the old tapes, rewriting the script, replacing the negative messages with positive ones.

When our wounded self says, "You're no good at that," we can counter with "I might be better at that than I think am."

We're not countering the blow with direct force but redirecting the energy in a less destructive direction. Sort of mental aikido. We are just opening up to new possibilities. We can even counter with "Maybe I'm not so good now, but I can improve."

When the old tapes say, "That story is pathetic," we can counter with "That's okay. It's a work in progress. I am improving it with each revision."

If the story is already published with no way of changing it, we can counter with "Okay, but my next story will be better. Because I am a work in progress. It's one step on my author journey."

We are shifting from a message of shame to a message of progress and hope.

Besides paying attention to our self-talk, we need to pay attention to our feelings of resistance when we sit down to write. These feelings that bubble up when we are drafting or revising are important. They can fuel a writing session or sabotage it. It's helpful to sort out what our feelings are telling us and whether we need to forge ahead or pause and do healing work.

Are you uncertain where the story is going? Are you questioning your ability to come up with the next scene or wrap up the story threads? Is the tension in the scene simply getting a little much for you? Is something in the story triggering old traumas for you?

You may need to take a break and catch your breath. Or you might meditate or freewrite or journal before you get back to writing. Breathing in positive creative energy then releasing negativity and fear on the out-breath. Creative energy in, negativity out.

Sometimes I find myself really tense in the middle or approaching the climax of a story. Not because of self-doubt but because I've put my main character in jeopardy and am worried for her. I know that sounds silly, but I let myself feel what my character is feeling. I imagine how I'd feel in their situation, like method acting but for writing. Doing this can be emotionally draining. I have literally cried when writing and editing emotionally charged scenes, like when a beloved character dies.

When this is what's happening, take frequent breaks and chill between scenes. Or switch to a funny or lighthearted scene. Some of my funniest scenes are when everything is going to hell for my main character. Providing some laughter in a tense scene not only helps you in the writing process, but it provides relief for the reader as well.

I wrote a scene in one of my Jinx Ballou books in which Jinx is at the end of her rope, struggling to deal with a major trauma. She's considering suicide. It's a dark, dark scene. And just when she starts seriously considering ending her life, her dog Diana walks up and starts licking her face. Big sloppy golden retriever kisses. Jinx gets grossed out at first and then realizes she wants to live. She laughs and gives Diana a big hug for saving her life.

Whenever you feel that resistance while sitting at the keyboard, pay attention to it. Maybe you're not sure exactly what's going on. And that's okay. You don't have to turn it into a major therapy session each time you open your laptop. You can simply acknowledge it. "Hey, I'm feeling a little tense. Sensing a little resistance, some apprehension about writing this scene. But I will get through this."

If the resistance gets unbearable or keeps you from writing, use the tools in this book to work through it and then dive back in at a pace that feels comfortable. Just start writing. If the right words aren't coming, then put in the wrong words. If you're not sure how to write this scene, if you're feeling some hesitancy, just write it as best you can. It's always easier to edit a rough draft than a blank page. Always.

22

Sitting with the Fear and Self-Doubt

As I stated in the last chapter, sometimes we aren't sure where our resistance or self-doubt comes from when we sit down to write. Maybe no matter how much we meditate and use affirmations and journal and freewrite, our inner troll is screaming at us that we can't do it, that no one will want to read what we're writing.

This negativity can be frustrating. We're doing everything we can to silence this voice of shame. But it just will not shut the hell up. Yeah, I've been there. Most of us have.

And if we are writing for a living, the pressure is on. If our latest book isn't selling, if the readthrough in our series isn't where we hoped it would be, if our publisher doesn't extend our current series or closes up shop entirely, if our agent quits the business to work on their own writing, if, if, if... It's not as if the power company or our mortgage company will say, "Don't worry about it—we'll wait."

Sometimes, there's no choice but to sit with the fear

and self-doubt. We just have to let ourselves feel whatever our inner troll is feeling. To acknowledge that we are questioning whether we have what it takes to be a "real" writer. We're afraid that we will fail or that the world will find out that we're an imposter. We're afraid that if this next chapter of our rough draft isn't perfect, isn't in the right character's voice, is tainted by info dumps and plot holes, that we'll never be able to fix it.

Sometimes, we just have to sit right down there in the mud, letting the uncomfortable emotions ooze around our soul. We sit and breathe and feel the unpleasant emotions. The fear, the frustrations, the despair, the shame, whatever it is.

As I mentioned earlier in the book, the troll inside of us, our shaming voice, isn't bad. It's where we are wounded. It's the frightened child within us. While it is spewing all of this shame and fear and negativity, all it really wants is to be heard and acknowledged.

Sometimes we just have to sit with it and say, "I hear you. I understand why you're afraid. I understand why you feel ashamed. I understand why every critique or negative review cuts you to the quick. You've been hurt before, and you're afraid of being hurt again."

Sometimes, instead of pushing our inner troll aside, we simply need to embrace it. Doing this won't necessarily make it go away. But over time, it can make it less able to rob us of our joy of writing.

By acknowledging the emotions, we are being proactive. Once we've let ourselves embrace the feelings, we can say, "I've heard you. Now let's move forward and create anyway. If we make mistakes, we will fix them. If we receive negative feedback, we will handle it because we will get positive feedback too. And if one project flops, then we'll take the lessons from that and do something better next time."

A good way to do this is with meditation. One of the

goals of meditation is to pay attention, to be here now. We acknowledge the thoughts and feelings that arise. We don't fight them. We breathe in, acknowledge them, and then release them. And as more thoughts and emotions arise, even the same ones we just released, we acknowledge them and release them. Over and over.

Gradually, we see that the troll is just our frightened inner child in a Halloween costume. We embrace that part of us, hearing it out, and together release all of the negativity as it arises.

We dismantle the fear and shame by honoring where these feelings came from and recognizing that we can move past them. Yes, we may have been humiliated by a teacher or parent or spouse who didn't see the value in our writing. We may have been crushed by an unduly harsh editor who told us we didn't have what it took to be a writer.

But we are getting better. We are finding good stuff in our writing. We no longer have to live in shame or fear. We can be here now. We can move forward, improving with every story we write, recognizing not only the flaws in our work but the gems there as well.

23

Nonattachment to Your Work

Early in our author journey, our writing feels like an essential extension of our being. We may call our stories our babies. They are so precious to us. We put so much raw emotion into them. We made ourselves vulnerable by telling these stories. We went out on a limb, trying something so new and outside our comfort zone.

When we get feedback on these early attempts, even if it's well-intentioned and constructive, it can feel like someone stomping all over our very souls. Someone told us our babies were ugly and not fit to be seen in public.

Over time, as we finish more stories, the constructive critiques hurt less. But we can still be vulnerable to harsh reviews, especially if they are from industry reviewers. And the random one-star review on Amazon can continue to feel like a knife to the heart.

We may no longer consider these stories to be our babies, but they are still a product of our imagination and creativity. We worked hard to make them as polished and entertaining as we could. And then when we read that we missed the mark and came up short, at least in the mind of this reviewer, all of that shame we used to feel from a critique comes flooding back.

"I'm just not good enough," we may think. "I'm a failure."

As I mentioned in the chapter on reviews, what someone else says about us (or our work) is none of our business. Remember, it's just one person's opinion. If it turns out to be a widely held opinion, well, that's a different story, which I will deal with in the next chapter.

But the odd negative review is one person's opinion, as mentioned in the chapter on reviews. They aren't written for us but for readers.

That doesn't mean we can't feel disappointed. We're still human beings. We like to learn that something we spent months or even years creating is reaching readers and delivering the entertainment value we envisioned for it. We like praise and don't like criticism.

The same goes for sales numbers. Whenever we launch a new book, we have such high hopes, especially on launch day. We want to see daily sales in the thousands and tens of thousands. But then we discover it only sold twelve copies on day one, only a few dozen in the first month. We panic and question everything. The book. Our career. Our life.

"Why aren't people buying my book? What's wrong with it? Is it the cover? The book description? Did people hate the last book and give up on me as an author?"

Buddhism has a concept called "nonattachment," also known as "detachment" in psychology circles. It has a lot of different definitions, but basically, nonattachment is a process of letting go. We are letting go of how external events affect our serenity. We are letting go of any emotional attachment between the outside world and our sense of worth.

We put a lot of time and energy and thought into our stories. They are the hard-earned product of our creativity.

But they are not us. Our stories are not sentient. They are simply a collection of ideas and words. They are an arrangement of the same twenty-six letters that Herman Melville used to tell *Moby-Dick*, that Dr. Seuss used to tell *Green Eggs and Ham*, that Barbara Cartland used to tell steamy romances, and that Robert Ludlum used to tell *The Bourne Identity*. They are impermanent. They have no inherent worth outside of what any individual assigns to them.

Our worth as human beings and as authors is not determined by what other people say about our stories. Our worth has no connection to our sales numbers. Our worth isn't in question. And because our worth is never in question, we can detach from what other people say about our stories. We can let go of the need to validate ourselves as writers from awards and bestseller labels.

We can practice nonattachment through meditation. When we sit, we can imagine ourselves with the pages of our stories in hand. And then we can imagine letting those pages go and flying all around the world to land in the hands of readers and reviewers.

The important thing is the letting go. We are not simply releasing our writing into the world. We are letting it go. Letting go of our attachment to it. Letting go of our attachment to how many people buy the book and how they experience it when they read it.

We have already put everything we can into it. We have given it our best. Now the pages are free to fly away into the breeze of publication. Away they go, and with them goes all emotional connection to them. We wish them well, but we are moving on to enjoying creating the next story.

Breathe in peace and joy and gratitude for being able to create the story. Exhale and release your attachment to the stories. As our chest relaxes and the air exits our lungs, so goes all connection to the stories, all connection to what anyone may say about them, all connection to how many people buy them and read them.

If emotional attachment to your work troubles you, do this meditation every day and see how your feelings change over time. Keep letting go. Keep detaching. Whatever happens, whatever anyone says, our worth as authors and as human beings remains unaffected. We are still growing and learning and improving our craft with every story we write.

You can also incorporate nonattachment into your affirmations.

My worth as a writer is not in question.

The reviews that my books receive do not determine my worth as a writer.

Sales numbers do not correlate to the quality of my work.

I do not have to be a bestseller to be a good writer.

I am a good writer and take pride in my work.

A negative review does not make me a bad writer.

I let go of my emotional attachment to book sales and reviews.

Reviews of my work have nothing to do with my worth as a writer.

You can word these affirmations however you want. You may need to soften them with willingness or readiness.

I am willing to see reviews differently.

I am willing to let go of my attachment to reviews and ratings.

I am ready to accept that my worth as a writer isn't determined by reviews.

I am willing to be proud of my writing no matter how many copies it sells.

I am ready to be at peace with my author journey and let go of my attachment to sales and reviews.

We may still resist letting go of our attachment to reviews and sales. But we are willing. We are ready to change and be free from the emotional ties to our work. We are open to getting off the emotional roller coaster.

Letting go will take time. Our instinct will be to keep grabbing it because that shaming voice persists in telling us that our worth is tied to our work. But if we keep letting go, in time, we can develop a healthy detachment and enjoy our author journey more.

24

Dealing with Failures and Flops

Failure is always an option. We're not sending astronauts into the vacuum of space. We are telling stories.

There are no guarantees. No guarantee that our editor will like the story. No guarantee we will get glowing reviews. No guarantee how many books we will sell. No guarantee of any awards. Failure is always an option.

The thought of our current project not meeting expectations can fill us with fear.

Sometimes it's not just one review that sends us into an emotional tailspin. Sometimes a book outright flops. Despite all the time, effort, and thought we've put into it. Despite everything our editing team put into making it as perfect as it can be. Sometimes a book just doesn't resonate with readers. Sometimes an entire series, a passion project, can be met with crickets.

This failure can be especially hard if we experienced success with an early novel but subsequent books barely move the needle. We may wonder if we're just a flash in the pan, a one-hit wonder doomed to spend the rest of our author journey in obscurity with the rest of us poor schlubs. Welcome to the cheap seats, buddy.

Or maybe we've had a series of bestsellers, but then the winds change. Without warning, what was super popular is now passé. The crowds have moved on to the next big thing.

Such is the nature of the author's journey and the literary world in general. One year, vampires are the big thing. Next year, it's moody crime fiction with unreliable narrators. Then it's YA magic school fiction, military sci-fi, cozy mysteries, or mermaids. I'm still waiting for mermaids to be popular.

Literary trends do not an author career make. And while you may get lucky by getting the right book to the right publisher at the right time, and they put a gazillion dollars into marketing it to just the right subset of readers, you can't count on that always being the case.

I'm currently reading Peter Benchley's *The Deep*, his follow-up to his debut blockbuster novel *Jaws*. It's awesome. If you're as old as I am, you remember what a splash (sorry, couldn't help myself) his first two novels made. Not only were they mega bestsellers (dare I say, beach reads?), but the movies they spawned (I don't know what's gotten into me) blew up like Bruce the shark (sorry, spoilers) or a reef full of artillery shells.

Peter Benchley was the guy who had readers turning pages, especially since they were now afraid to go into the water. So, what other blockbusters did he write? Well, there was *The Island*. The book did okay, but the movie they made from it tanked. And then there was *The Girl of the Sea of Cortez*, *Q Clearance*, and *Rummies*. Ever heard of them? No? Neither had I, until I looked up his bibliography.

He followed up those three with *Beast*, about a killer genetically engineered giant squid, and *White Shark* (later retitled *Creature*), which was not actually about a shark but a Nazi-engineered human-amphibian-monster creature.

Were these books inferior to *Jaws* and *The Deep*? I doubt it. I haven't read them, but experience tells me his skills improved over time. But for whatever reason, the subsequent books weren't the mega bestsellers his previous works were. Maybe they didn't get the right marketing. Maybe readers had just moved on.

Was he a failure? No.

Eventually, Benchley shifted his focus to educating people about sharks as remarkable creatures rather than the mindless monsters he originally portrayed them as. He became an activist to protect the many species of sharks, in part to undo the damage that *Jaws* did. No, his activism may not have garnered him the attention that his earlier adventure thrillers did, but I'm sure it was satisfying work.

Now I've really taken the wind out of your sails. Is your career doomed to sink beneath the briny waves before you've even left the dock? And with so many more authors writing, and more novels being published every year, what hope do you have of ever rising to the surface? Okay, enough with the marine puns.

Becoming an author that everyone's talking about is incredibly rare. You have a better shot at winning the lottery. Seriously, it's nice to dream, but we're all about getting grounded in reality here. If you hit it big, great. Don't count on that always being the case. If you never earn that bestseller status, so what?

Did we start writing to become a household name and sip champagne on our hundred-foot yacht? No. We started writing stories because we liked to write. We liked to create stories and characters and worlds. We liked to play with words. We liked playing "what if?"

If fame and fortune were what motivated you to write, I've got some bad news for you. Those lofty goals are nice but will not sustain a writing career. There are easier ways to make money.

To be a writer, you have to love writing. You have to love combining your creative voice with your editorial voice. You have to love telling stories. You have to love sitting down at your keyboard for hours at a time. Okay, fine, take breaks every hour or so. But then get back to it.

So, what happens when a book we had such high hopes for launches to the sound of crickets? How do we cope when a story that we've put our heart and soul into gets ripped to shreds by professional reviewers and readers alike? Is it time to hang it all up? Hell no!

So much of we do is experimenting and exploring, pushing our writing skills to the limits. And sometimes those experiments strike gold. Most times, they do okay. And occasionally, we find that our latest novel or series was a dud. That's okay. Learn what you can from what went wrong and move on.

A flop doesn't make you a failure. It doesn't mean you're a terrible writer. It doesn't make you an imposter if you were fortunate enough to win an award for an earlier work. No one is coming to take back your award. It's yours. You earned it. Now keep writing.

Maybe we have developed a brand for writing sword-and-sorcery fantasy, and then we write a steampunk romance that has our devoted fans screaming with rage and disappointment. Or maybe we experimented and tried writing in present tense, only to learn that it didn't resonate with our readers. Whatever the reason, it doesn't mean we're a talentless hack. It's not as if our mojo has suddenly evaporated.

When this happens to you, it's time to reassess and face whatever insecurities may be coming up. Our creative self-doubt can have a field day with these situations if we let it. But we don't have to let it.

We have the tools outlined earlier to work through these feelings and negative self-talk. We have meditation, affirmations, and journaling. If we get stuck and can't figure out what to write next (because the troll in our head is sure that our next story will tank even worse), we can always just freewrite until something sparks.

At times like this, we need to be extra gentle with our author selves. These blows can definitely leave some bruises on our ego. It can help to share our experiences and feelings with other authors. No doubt you will find you are not alone. Building a career as writer can be tough. In fact, I'd dare to say that the business side of writing is much harder than the writing side. And that's saying something.

Author careers have ups and downs. The publishing business is always changing. Publishers merge or go out of business. Indie authors are pushing boundaries and opening up new opportunities for marginalized voices. Amazon is always changing their rules. New retailers and distributors appear or vanish. New technology is always emerging.

In the past twenty years, we've seen e-books and audiobooks become a thing. Serialized fiction is catching on in the US. (and has been popular for a while in Asia). AI technology is impacting our world as well. Who knows what's next?

Learning to ride the waves instead of getting wiped out (aw, crap, I'm doing it again, aren't I?) isn't easy. It takes time. Don't be in a rush to quit your day job. Learn to detach from the numbers game and the fame game.

If one of your books suddenly goes viral, awesome. But don't get attached to that success. It may last a while, or it may be fleeting. Either way, just keep writing and being intentional about your love of writing. Trust your process. Let every day at the keyboard be an opportunity to indulge in playing "what if?"

25

Leveling Up

Leveling up is a topic we don't talk about much in author circles. At least not the ones I frequent. But it can leave an emerging author feeling a little awkward.

Several years ago, I was a part of a small, informal critique group. We met every week to share what we'd written and to offer feedback. I loved going. Not only because I learned how to improve my writing, but I enjoyed just hanging with these friends. We were all starting out and learning the ropes together, cheering one another on, celebrating accomplishments.

I was not the first person in the group to get published. Closer to the third. But then I got an agent. And then a two-book publishing deal from one of the Big Five. And suddenly, I had editorial deadlines. I had standards to maintain. Playtime was over. I was a professional now. I had leveled up.

That was all fantastic, but it also meant that I needed to spend more time writing. I didn't have time for weekly critiques. I had six months to write, revise, and deliver my second novel to my editor. All while still doing my day job.

My attendance at the weekly critique group became less and less frequent until I realized I just didn't have the time. I loved my friends. They were such awesome people. But leveling up meant dropping out of the group and focusing on my author career. I still have some sadness about it. I miss hanging with them.

This happens sometimes. And every author's journey is unique. We all have different demands on our time. We have to make the decisions that are right for us. But my point in this chapter is to let you know that sometimes, leveling up means we have to decide where and how we show up. Where we put our time. Whom we spend time with.

I am not suggesting that leveling up means you have to become a hermit doing nothing but writing and going to your day job. Maintaining a healthy social life can be a buoy for the ups and downs of the author journey. Maybe you don't need to quit your favorite critique group or your professional writer organization. But you need to balance your commitments.

As an indie author, I have to worry not only about getting my manuscript to my editor on time but also managing ads, scheduling interviews and podcast appearances, fulfilling orders from my website, attending author events, etc. It's a lot of demand on my time. With each title I release, the demands only increase.

If you have a publisher, maybe they will handle some of these responsibilities. But even if they do, you will still need to show up to interviews and handle some of the marketing. You may have to field multiple opportunities or juggle several projects at once.

Leveling up is a good thing, but you have to be more mindful of what you say yes to and what you pass on. It may mean letting go of involvement in activities you previously enjoyed. It may mean taking on financial risks.

Leveling up can involve a sense of guilt. When I signed with my publisher, I feared (wrongfully, as it turned out) that my friends in the critique group would resent me. I didn't want them to think I had changed just because I now had this opportunity.

They didn't, of course. They were excited for me. They were happy about my success. That's what friends do.

The author journey is unique for each one of us. It's hard to know where it will take us next. Opportunities can come when we least expect them. Sometimes, we ache for opportunities that never materialize (such as movie deals, etc.).

Assess each opportunity carefully when it appears. Don't get starry-eyed by promises of glory. What will saying yes require of you? Are you able to meet those commitments? Will it require saying no to something else?

It's okay to say no to opportunities. If the deal is too good to be true, walk away. If it will require more than you can deliver, don't put yourself in a no-win situation. Can you outline, draft, and revise a full novel in the time allotted? What will you have to give up?

There are no right or wrong answers. Make the best choices you can. Live with the consequences of those choices. And level up when you're ready.

26

There Is No Silver Bullet

I listen to a lot of interviews with authors, including some who are making a boatload of cash. Six-figure authors who are absolutely killing it. And when I listen to these interviews, a part of me is desperate to learn their secret to success. What's the silver bullet? What's the magic formula?

That part of me is desperate to have the same level of success. And why not? Most of us want to make lots of money and say goodbye to our financial woes and our dreary day jobs.

But I have to remind myself that there is no silver bullet for success. No magical formula that will suddenly draw the attention of millions of readers who are desperate to buy my books.

The authors who break out suddenly are the exception to the rule. Sure, they are talented. They work hard. They've connected with a supportive fanbase that loves their work. But there was also a bit of luck involved. Maybe more than a bit.

I hear authors say that to be successful, you have to do this or do that. You have to run ads. You have to set your first book in a series to free. You have to do a BookBub Feature Deal. You have to be exclusive to Kindle Unlimited. You have to be wide. You have to have a newsletter with a gazillion subscribers and an open rate of sixty percent.

You have to write romance or YA or crime fiction or whatever the flavor of the week is. You have to use an outline. Or you have to write organically without an outline. You have to publish a book every month or two. Or that you shouldn't publish so frequently. You have to be traditionally published. You have to publish your own work.

In one podcast interview, an author will swear by one tactic. In the next episode of the same podcast, a different author will swear the opposite tactic is the only way to go.

It's easy to get whiplash listening to these authors, believing that they have the answers to your success. But they don't. Most have, at best, a vague understanding of their own success. I'm not trying to dismiss their success. I'm happy for them. Clearly, they have found fans who love their work. Unfortunately, duplicating that level of success is difficult, if not impossible.

When we flip back and forth, trying different tactics, it can trigger our creative self-doubt. Our inner troll tells us we'll never be successful. We're just not talented enough. We're not creative enough. We're not smart enough.

We can do certain things to improve the success of our author journey. Making sure the books we put out are as polished and engaging as we can make them is a must. And if we are going the self-publication route, it's important to make sure that our books are professionally edited, with professional covers that reflect our genre and book descriptions that are engaging and get readers to click that buy button. Writing in a series can improve readthrough. Some genres are more popular than others.

Creating a newsletter and figuring out how to provide content our subscribers enjoy and that gives more than it

THERE IS NO SILVER BULLET

asks is another crucial part of the success formula. That is no simple task. I'm still figuring that strategy out.

But beyond that, there are tactics that work for some but not others. This isn't math or science. It's very inexact. There are simply too many factors for results to duplicate themselves on a regular basis. Some people are good at certain tactics and find success there. While others find a completely different approach works better for them. And they all will swear that their way is the only way for success.

Stop looking for gurus who hold the secret to your success. That includes me. I don't know how to make your authorial career successful. I don't know how to make myself successful. We're all just figuring it out, and the rules are always changing. What may work like gangbusters for some for one month may not even move the needle for the same people a few months later.

I'm constantly seeing posts in writers' groups online that essentially say, "My sales suddenly tanked in the past week. What happened? Did Amazon do something? Did IngramSpark do something? Is Facebook not showing my ads?"

And the responses range from "Yeah, mine dipped too" to "My sales are going up. Things are great."

It's not always possible to know why things suddenly improve or worsen for any given author or book using the tactics and strategies they are using. So don't drive yourself crazy. Uncouple your love of writing and your sense of worth as an author from sales numbers. And that's so hard to do.

Believe me. I'm desperate to be able to quit my day job and write full time. I'm hungry for all the success and accolades. But every day that I can write for at least half an hour is a good day.

There is no silver bullet. The gurus who claim that this tactic or that is *the* way to be successful are full of beans. For every successful author who has hit gold using a specific tactic, there are thousands of others using the same tactic with minimal results.

Write the books you want to write. Write them with love and passion. Enjoy the process. Polish them as best you can with help from professionals. Publish them. Do what feels authentic to you to find readers who are a good fit for your work. Engage with these readers in a way that is genuine and that makes them love spending time in your universe. And then trust the process.

This strategy may make you a lot of money. It may not. But this approach allows you to enjoy the act of writing and connecting with people who are passionate about your work. It helps to keep the creative self-doubt at bay.

Because if you're only in it for the money, go sell real estate or some other profession. Writing isn't about money, though the money helps. Writing is about creativity and joy and love and passion. It's about connecting with others and telling stories that mean something to you.

27

Getting Professional Help

Dealing with creative self-doubt may require more than the tools offered in this book. Your creative self-doubt may be part of a deeper issue. Sometimes, you may need professional help. And there is no shame in getting help when you need it.

I've been on antidepressants and related medications in the past, especially when I was undergoing my gender transition back in the 1990s and dealing with widespread discrimination and abandonment. I was in an abusive relationship. And I was drinking and using other unhealthy coping mechanisms to deal.

I hit bottom when I attempted to end my life, not because I wanted to die but because I could no longer stand to live in such emotional pain all the time. Fortunately, I survived. And I got help. I started going to Alcoholics Anonymous and several other twelve-step programs. I started going to therapy. I went on antidepressants and other meds for a few years.

Eventually, I weaned off the meds as I became emotionally stronger and able to use healthy coping mechanisms to deal with daily challenges and work through my past trauma. I thought that would be the last time I would need such help. I was wrong.

During the writing of this book, I've had to go back on medication to help me deal with anxiety and panic attacks. This anxiety is tied to my long history of financial-related trauma and a series of large, unexpected expenses at home that I've been struggling to figure out how to meet. But this time, I was at least armed with the wisdom of knowing I could get help.

I am privileged in being able to get help. Not everyone has access to affordable healthcare, especially mental healthcare. I wish I had an easy answer for those without these options. If you do not have access, be proactive to search out what resources may be available to you.

As I said, my first decision was to go to Alcoholics Anonymous. It is a free group. Yes, they pass the hat at meetings, but if you can't contribute, no one will look down their nose at you. And yes, they talk a lot about God or Higher Powers. There are also other groups geared toward helping people struggling with substance abuse and other problems that take a different, more secular approach.

If you can't find a group that suits your needs, consider starting one. A group in which it is safe to be authentic and vulnerable.

For years, I was a part of a group of women that came together each week to share what was going on in our lives. It was an informal group of women from all different backgrounds, age groups, racial backgrounds, and sexualities. Some of us were addicts. Others weren't. We had no set agenda. That group fed my soul in ways that therapy and twelve-step groups couldn't.

If you have a substance abuse problem, get help. If you are struggling with mental health issues, get help however you can. If you are feeling suicidal, call a helpline. I've listed some in the resources section of this book. At the very least, find a way to connect with other human beings in an honest way.

Getting help when you need it can save your life. It can help you find more joy. And it can help you reconnect with your love for writing. As I said before, many of the tools I have shared in this book have come from my recovery. I share them because they worked for me and many others. Take what you like and leave the rest.

28

Changing Course and Walking Away

Writing isn't for everyone. Just as music and sports and video games aren't for everyone. You may eventually decide writing isn't for you. Maybe, despite all that I've shared, you simply can't muster up any joy or love when you sit down at the keyboard to write. You may be dealing with life situations that simply don't allow you to write. Maybe you have a significant other who is so nonsupportive that it is creating friction in your relationship.

It may be time to walk away from writing. I don't say that lightly. Don't give up without at least trying the tools I've shared here.

Maybe writing just isn't a good fit for how your brain works. I tried my hand at music and painting when I was younger. But I always felt I was missing something essential. I couldn't look at a sheet of music and hear it in my head. I hated practicing scales. As much as I enjoyed playing guitar, I couldn't muster up enough passion to keep going. My brain just wasn't a good fit for that medium of creativity.

The same went for painting. I love to watch Bob Ross create his beautiful artwork. My mother was a painter and a graphic designer. And while I can create book covers and web graphics, I am not a painter. I can't draw for crap. Seeing something and then trying to re-create it on paper or canvas or any other media is not something my brain knows how to do. It's simply not wired that way.

I walked away from writing for decades. I was super passionate about writing as a teenager. I pored over *Writer's Market* to find places to submit my stories, read every article in *Writer's Digest* to improve my craft. I attended two creative writing classes in college.

But after college, I lost interest as my gender issues dominated my life. It wasn't until twenty years later that I once again expressed an interest in writing.

Realizing that a form of creativity isn't a good fit isn't a failure. It's simply a revelation. It's a step toward something else that may fulfill you in ways you never imagined. Me walking away from painting and eventually music opened the door for me to fall back in love with writing. And I realized that my brain is very much wired for the written word. It isn't so much about talent as it is compatible brain function. Or maybe that's what talent is.

Maybe you love writing but aren't passionate about what you are writing. Maybe instead of walking away from writing entirely, all you need to do is change course. Try a different genre or form. If you're writing romance but feeling unfulfilled, try science fiction or mystery or urban fantasy. If you're tired of the limitations of YA, try writing adult fiction. Maybe instead of prose, you could give poetry or screenwriting a gander.

Switch from fiction to nonfiction or vice versa. I know

a few people who have switched from writing mysteries and thrillers to writing true crime. And they love it.

This is your journey. Don't spend it doing something that makes you miserable. No one is forcing you to be a writer. No one is forcing you to write in a specific genre or format. Even if writing is your profession, maybe it's time to consider new directions. You can always come back to it.

Change course or walk away to something more fulfilling. No one will think less of you. Except maybe your mom. But hey, you can't please everybody. The best you can do is please yourself. You deserve to be happy.

29

Final Thoughts and Parting Shots

This is your author journey. You may not control how much money you make. But you decide what to write, how fast you write, and how you write. You decide how your work gets published or if you want to publish at all. You decide whether to make it a grueling experience or a joyful act of creativity. You decide if the time has come to walk away. And if you do walk away, you have the option to return like I did.

Whatever you do, do it with love. Do it with passion. Enjoy the journey. Writing is hard work, but it doesn't have to be miserable work. Work and joy are not mutually exclusive.

Writing can be a way for you to connect with all kinds of amazing people, including readers, fellow authors, and other industry professionals. I have come to relish the friendships I have developed in this global community of writers.

I read a lot of amazing stories and have learned a lot about how different people experience the world. We are social creatures, and writing is an essential way we connect.

And when we connect, deeply and authentically, the world can seem much less dark. It can be a world of love and stories.

Here are my final thoughts that I want to leave you with.

Many writers struggle with creative self-doubt.

Creation is messy.

Trust the process.

Trust *your* process.

Allow for change and growth.

Be willing to see things differently.

You are not an imposter. You are an amazing creative human being.

Avoid extreme thinking and embrace the Middle Way.

Reclaim your love of writing.

Let go of your attachment to reviews or success. Focus on the work.

Be gentle with yourself and your work.

Finish the projects you start.

Don't be afraid to level up.

Focus on progress, not perfection.

You've got this! Now break through.

Now, the next chapter in this book is a list of resources that I have found helpful and think you will too. But before we get to that, there is something I need to ask you.

Remember when I mentioned at the beginning of this book that creative self-doubt is ubiquitous in the author community? And not just for authors—for all creatives, including actors, musical artists, visual artists, etc.

So many of us are struggling with this issue, and it is strangling our careers. These people need help breaking through their own creative self-doubt. And you can make that happen. You can help them. Remember how I said that helping authors also helps you? Here's your chance.

If you have gotten anything out of this book, please

FINAL THOUGHTS AND PARTING SHOTS

share it with your fellow authors. Mention it in your writers' groups, on social media and in person. Help them connect not only with the ideas in this book that helped both you and me but also to the resources I share in the next chapter.

We are a community of writers who are changing the world. By spreading the word, you are fueling that change. Thank you in advance from the bottom of my heart.

30

Resources

I've compiled a list of resources that have helped me with creative self-doubt, anxiety, and more serious issues, including substance abuse, codependency, and suicidal ideation. This is far from a comprehensive list. These are resources that I have personal experience with (with a few minor exceptions). They helped me. I believe that they have the power to help you too.

Each of us faces our challenges with a unique mindset and history of experiences. There is no shortage of books on creativity and overcoming mental blocks. There are countless videos and YouTube channels and podcasts related to this topic. But perhaps this chapter can be a starting point for you. Feel free to reach out to fellow authors for their recommendations. Together, we can do greater.

Because links don't always show up well in books, I've created a page on my website where you can find links to all of these resources.

Visit dharmakelleher.com/breakthrough-links.

Books

The Artist's Way
Julia Cameron

I discovered *The Artist's Way* when I was a member of a private women's support group. It's been around for twenty-five years and has helped countless creative people discover their passion and channel their creativity. It is a great resource for helping you fill your creative well by not only inspiring you but giving you concrete homework assignments that yield results.

Women Who Run with the Wolves: Myths and Stories of the Wild Woman Archetype
Clarissa Pinkola Estés

This was another book I fell in love with as a member of the women's group. *Women Who Run with the Wolves* is a deep anthropological dive into the power of storytelling and personal growth. Estés explores the origins and meanings of classic teaching stories from a variety of cultures and takes them apart.

Why would this benefit you? It helps to understand why different types of stories resonate with different people and sheds light on the impact our words can have.

Eat Pray Love: One Woman's Search for Everything Across Italy, India and Indonesia
Elizabeth Gilbert

Eat Pray Love is one woman's search for meaning and passion. For Gilbert, this journey was a major leap of faith. What I hope you get out of this book is the understanding that your pursuit of writing and the passion associated with it is a journey. One filled with taking chances, setbacks, and growing from one stage to the next in expected and unexpected ways.

This book helped shape my perspective of my own creative journey. It prepared me to better learn from my failures, gave me courage to walk away from situations and people that did not serve my needs and to continue to strive for better.

I am just now reading Gilbert's follow-up book, *Big Magic: Creative Living Beyond Fear*. This one is more prescriptive than *Eat Pray Love*. Although I haven't finished it, I believe it's on par with Cameron's *The Artist's Way*. So check it out.

THE PRACTICE: SHIPPING CREATIVE WORK
Seth Godin

I've been a fan of Seth Godin for many, many years. His books *Permission Marketing* and *All Marketers Are Liars* (later retitled *All Marketers Tell Stories*) were groundbreaking for me when I was a freelance web developer. Especially because I am an introvert, for a long time, the concept of marketing scared the snot out of me. Long story short, it doesn't anymore, thanks in large part to what I've learned from Seth Godin.

His book *The Practice*, however, really spoke to me as an author. As the title suggests, the book focuses on our practice as creatives. It helps us realize the ways in which we have been sabotaging our author journey and shows us how to change our perspective to better serve our readers while building our author brand.

I also want to recommend his earlier book *This is Marketing: You Can't Be Seen Until You Learn to See*. Many of the same concepts but with a slightly different slant. If you struggle with marketing (and who of us doesn't?), read both of these books.

The Successful Author Mindset: A Handbook for Surviving the Writer's Journey
Joanna Penn

I discovered Joanna Penn's *The Creative Penn* podcast way back before my first book was published by Random House. She is one of the pioneers from the early days of self-publishing. She gave me the courage and knowledge to walk away from traditional publishing and go indie.

In addition to her crime fiction series, she has written several books for writers, most notably *The Successful Author Mindset*. She touches on several of the issues we have explored together in this book, as well as many others. Whether you are pursuing the trad pub route or the indie pub route, you will find it an invaluable resource.

I'd also recommend the book she cowrote with Dr. Euan Lawson, *The Healthy Writer: Reduce Your Pain, Improve Your Health, and Build a Writing Career for the Long Term*. It deals with helping you avoid a range of pitfalls that can physically impact your writing career.

The 5 Second Rule: Transform Your Life, Work, and Confidence with Everyday Courage
Mel Robbins

I literally just finished reading this book ten minutes ago. But I'm here to tell you it is a game-changer. Her five-second rule will help you make better decisions, optimize your writing time, avoid missed opportunities, and empower you to overcome the habits sabotaging your author journey. Don't skip this one.

Podcasts

I listen to a lot of podcasts. They are an amazing resource for learning craft, sharing ideas, building relationships, and many other fantastic things. Here are some of my favorites I think you will enjoy. They should be all available on your podcatcher of choice, including Apple, Stitcher, Google, Spotify, etc.

Affirmation Meditation Podcast
Bob Baker

I listen to this podcast every morning immediately after getting out of bed and feeding the cat. I highly recommend listening. It will rewire your brain for the better. Baker also has a YouTube channel worth checking out.

The Creative Penn
Joanna Penn

As mentioned above, Joanna Penn is one of the pioneers in the indie author space. Whether you're trad-pubbed or indie, you will get a lot out of her podcast episodes.

AskALLi
The Alliance of Independent Authors

If you are an independent author or are considering self-publishing, then there is no better industry organization or resource than the Alliance of Independent Authors. However, you do not need to be a paid member to listen to their amazing podcast, which helps authors stay up-to-date on the latest industry information.

Next Level Authors
Sacha Black and Daniel Willcocks

Looking to level up your author business? Check

out Sacha and Danny on the *Next Level Authors* podcast. Tons of resources and ideas for stepping up your game and holding yourself accountable.

A word of warning—frequent f-bombs in this podcast. So if profanity offends you, it's okay to pass on this one. But you will be missing out on some fantastic wisdom.

The Sell More Books Show
Bryan Cohen and H. Claire Taylor

This is another fantastic resource for staying abreast of the ever-changing world of book publishing, as well as getting ideas for how to market your work. No profanity in this one, but Bryan is notorious for his use of eyeroll-worthy, dad joke–level puns. You've been warned.

I Should Be Writing
Mur Lafferty

What I love most about *I Should Be Writing* is Mur's down-to-earth honesty. She shares her struggles, both external and internal, with no sugarcoating whatsoever. And she's written some amazing books, including the novelization of the *Star Wars* movie *Solo*. Definitely worth a listen.

Ditch Diggers
Mur Lafferty and Matt Wallace

This podcast, while also hosted by Mur Lafferty, is more lighthearted than *I Should Be Writing*. But every episode includes a great discussion on the business of writing.

The Chase Jarvis LIVE Show
Chase Jarvis

Chase Jarvis is a professional photographer who interviews other creatives at the top of their game, as well as marketing experts. He discusses the ins and outs of being a professional creative, including mindset, how to price your work, etc. He, too, has a YouTube channel.

YouTube

I've included links to several YouTube videos that get to the heart of creative self-doubt. I've also included links to the channels on which they appear. Check them out.

CHASE JARVIS
"Seth Godin: Imposter Syndrome, Getting Unstuck and The Practice"

AUTHOR LEVEL UP (MICHAEL LA RONN)
"How to BEAT Self-Doubt"
"We Need to Talk About Fear and Self-Doubt"

BOB BAKER
"10 Most Powerful Affirmations of All Time"

TED
"How you can use imposter syndrome to your benefit"; Cannon-Brookes, Mike

TEDX TALKS
"The Surprising Solution to the Imposter Syndrome"; Solomon, Lou
"Defeating the inner imposter that keeps us from being successful"; Ford, Knatokie

Apps

I Am (from Monkey Taps)

I mentioned this app earlier. I highly recommend it. It's free on both Apple and Google.

Meetup.com

If you're looking to connect with other authors in your local community, especially if you are seeking a critique group, you may find success by joining Meetup.com. Every city is different, so your mileage may vary, as they say. But it's always a great place to start.

Spotify Playlists

Looking to get your groove on while you write? Here are some playlists that might suit your style.

Meditation Music 2021

Compiled by Meditation Station
Nice New Age instrumental music idea for writing, studying, relaxing.

Deep Focus

Compiled by Spotify
This is another great playlist to give you a little nondistracting background noise.

Movie Soundtracks and Cinematic Music

Compiled by Tobias Schneider
If you prefer writing to music from your favorite movies, give this playlist a listen.

BLUES GUITAR INSTRUMENTALS

Compiled by Darrell Robinson

Looking for something with a little more energy but still no distracting vocals? Check out this collection of blues instrumentals.

YOU GOT THIS

Compiled by Dharma Kelleher

I compiled this playlist of popular uplifting tunes for when you need an emotional boost or a reminder that you have what it takes to be a writer.

Organizations

THE ALLIANCE OF INDEPENDENT AUTHORS

https://www.allianceindependentauthors.org/

As mentioned above, this is the best industry organization worldwide for authors who choose to publish their own work. They have a wide range of resources to help you make the best decisions for your publishing journey, keep you up-to-date on the changing industry, and provide you discounts for a wide variety of vetted service providers.

NATIONAL NOVEL WRITING MONTH

https://nanowrimo.org/

Can you write a fifty-thousand-word novel in thirty days? Take the challenge. NaNoWriMo is what lured me back into the world of creative writing in 2007. It's a hell of a personal challenge that takes place not only in November but throughout the year.

Alcoholics Anonymous

https://www.aa.org/

Let's get real here. Some of us need help to stop drinking. The romantic notions of the drunk genius authors of old are tired. AA saved my ass. It's not for everyone, but I wouldn't be alive without it.

SMART Recovery

https://www.smartrecovery.org/

As I mentioned above, AA is not for everyone, particularly if the God/Higher Power issue is a major turnoff. I have no personal experience with SMART Recovery, but I know others who have had success with it. If you can't stop drinking and AA isn't your bag, try this instead.

Al-Anon

https://al-anon.org/

Maybe you're not an alcoholic, but a spouse, parent, or other loved one is. If that's the case, you may find Al-Anon a helpful resource. It's not a place to bitch about our loved one's drinking or other destructive behaviors. It's a 12-step program for taking control of our own lives.

Codependents Anonymous

https://coda.org/

Yes, this is another 12-step program. In my recovery, I realized that not only did I have a problem with drinking but also with attaching myself to unhealthy relationships. I sought my self-worth in how other people treated me, which was usually not so good. I found this program to be of great benefit.

Adult Children of Alcoholics

https://adultchildren.org/

If your parents are or were alcoholics, you may find a lot of wisdom and healing in the rooms of ACOA. I know I did.

Suicide and Crisis Hotlines

Suicide is no joke. I survived two attempts. If I had succeeded, I would have missed out on so much. And you would not be reading this book. If you need help, reach out.

National Suicide Prevention Lifeline (US): (800) 273-8255

The Trevor Project (for LGBTQ Youth): https://www.thetrevorproject.org/

Trans Lifeline (US): (877) 565-8860

Suicide Hotlines and Crisis Lines (UK): https://www.therapyroute.com/article/suicide-hotlines-and-crisis-lines-in-the-united-kingdom

Index

Adult Children of Alcoholics, 192
affirmations, 21–24
  and nonattachment, 154
  apps, 26, 190
  defined, 21
  examples, 22-23, 28-30, 32, 94-95, 123, 154
  resistance, 23, 26-28
Al-Anon, 192
Alcoholics Anonymous, 49, 63, 104, 171-172, 192
Allende, Isabel, 89
Alliance of Independent Authors, 11, 92, 187, 191
Amazon, 64, 67, 71, 86, 91, 103, 113, 151, 161
apps, 190
  I Am, 26, 190
  Meetup.com, 11, 97, 190
author voice, 88-89
author journey, 6-7, 14, 22, 24, 37, 50, 63-64, 81, 93, 113, 143, 151, 154-155, 158, 164-165, 168, 179
awards, 2, 10, 12, 48, 50, 64, 67, 71, 87, 93, 111-112, 114-116, 142, 153, 157, 160
Awkwafina, 9
Baker, Bob, 187, 189

Beginner's Mind, 79-81
Benchley, Peter, 158-159
Black, Sacha, 187-188
books, recommended, 184-186
brainstorming, 39, 54, 57-58, 80, 121, 123
Buddhism, 72, 79, 152
building community, 47, 190
burnout, 46, 60, 125, 137-140
Cameron, Julia, 38, 184
Child, Lee, 89
Christie, Agatha, 69, 89
Codependents Anonymous, 192
Cohen, Bryan, 188
Colbert, Stephen, 9-10, 69, 115
comparing yourself to others, 2, 26, 29, 53, 89-95
control, 63-67, 103-104, 116, 179
creative process, 42, 51-62, 64, 140
creative self-doubt, 1-7, 9, 21-23, 30, 32-33, 35-36, 43, 47, 125, 127, 138-139, 142, 160, 168, 170-171, 180
   and affirmations 21-23
   and burnout, 138-139
   and failure, 160
   and writer's block, 125, 127
   tools for overcoming, 13-42
   videos about, 189
creative well, 125, 128, 131-135
critiques and critique groups, 11, 18, 31, 37, 47, 70-71, 97-101, 115, 148, 151-152, 163-165, 190
Ebert, Roger, 106
editors, 37, 59, 67, 70-71, 77, 79, 86, 93, 98-101, 138-139, 149, 157
education, 1, 31, 47, 49, 73, 88, 93, 95
Evanovich, Janet, 132

extreme thinking, 70-73, 180
failure, 1, 10, 27, 87, 140, 152, 157-161
feedback, 37, 47, 70-71, 78, 97-101, 151
Fey, Tina, 9
flow state, 40-41, 61, 83, 122, 124
forgiveness, 48-50
Foster, Jodie, 10
freewriting, 39-40, 54-55, 123, 127, 144, 147, 161
Gilbert, Elizabeth, 184
Godin, Seth, 64, 125, 185, 189
gratitude, 22, 36-38, 43, 50, 76, 115, 117, 153
Hanks, Tom, 9, 83
health, 23, 43-50, 62, 137-138, 186
I Am app, 22, 26, 190
imposter syndrome, 1-2, 6, 9-12, 22, 25, 70-71, 85, 95, 148, 160, 180, 189
indie author gold rush, 92
influence, 66
inner editor, 5-6, 45, 54, 56, 59, 99, 126-128, 160
inner troll, 6-7, 9-11, 13-14, 17, 23-28, 33, 44-46, 49, 73, 94-95, 103, 125, 128, 138, 143, 147-149, 161, 168
Iron Goddess, 54, 87, 100
Jarvis, Chase, 188-189
journaling, 38-40, 43, 127, 144, 161
joy, 3-4, 11-12, 14, 17, 19, 57, 59, 69, 79-80, 83-85, 95, 109, 115-117, 121, 124, 139, 148, 153, 170, 173, 179
King, Stephen, 89, 93, 140
Konrath, J. A., 92
Labrecque, Tammi, 116
Lady Gaga, 10
Lafferty, Mur, 188
leveling up, 163-165

Lord of the Rings, The, 104
Matrix, The, 2, 87
meditation, 3, 13-19, 43, 72, 108, 117, 127, 144, 148-149, 153-154, 160, 187, 190
mental health, 60, 138, 172
Middle Way, the, 69-76, 94, 180
misery conspiracy, 114-115
Morrison, Toni, 69, 89, 95
muse, 4-6, 41, 43, 45, 54, 56, 84, 99, 120, 125-129
National Novel Writing Month, 77, 191
New York Times, 2, 6, 73, 75, 104, 107, 114
Newsletter Ninja, 116
newsletters, 65, 116, 168
nonattachment, 151-155
Nyong'o, Lupita, 10
organizations, 11, 47, 92, 164, 191
 see also Alliance of Independent Authors
passion, 79-80, 85, 87-88, 90, 121, 123, 170, 176, 179
Patterson, James, 95
Penn, Joanna, 92, 186-187
perfection, 49, 75, 86, 127, 180
Pinkola Estés, Clarissa, 184
podcasts, 22, 59, 67, 111, 116, 123, 164, 168, 187-189
professional help, 139, 171-173
realness, 2, 12, 23, 27-28, 148
Reichs, Kathy, 127
resentments, 41, 48-50, 67, 165
resistance, 23-24, 26, 33, 55, 59, 73, 143, 145, 147, 154
reviews, 2-3, 14, 37, 48, 64-65, 67, 69, 71, 73, 75, 84, 86, 100, 103-109, 114, 148, 151-155, 157, 160, 180
revisions, 6, 23, 55-57, 79-80, 93, 101, 123
Reynolds, Ryan, 9
Robbins, Mel, 186

rough drafts, 3, 5, 23, 29, 37, 52-59, 70, 74, 79-80, 84, 89, 93, 101, 123-124, 126, 131, 143, 145, 148
Saldana, Zoe, 106
self-publishing, 66, 86, 92-93, 99, 104, 108, 111, 113, 161, 164, 186-187
self-talk, 29, 141-145, 160
Shelley, Mary, 104
shiny object syndrome, 119-124
Siskel, Gene, 106
SMART Recovery, 192
Sneak Previews, 106
Spotify playlists, 190
Stoker, Bram, 104, 132
Streep, Meryl, 9
substance abuse, 9, 11, 35,-37 115, 138, 170-172, 183, 192-193
success, 1-2, 10, 12, 26-27, 50, 64, 71-72, 103, 111-117, 157, 161, 167-170, 180, 186
suicide and crisis hotlines, 193
Tan, Amy, 89
Taylor, H. Claire, 188
TED talks, 189
Tolkien, J.R.R., 104
traditional publishing, 74, 79, 84, 86, 92-93, 99, 105, 107-108, 111, 113, 168
tropes, 65, 105, 107, 134
uncertainty, 1, 3, 30-31, 40, 52, 71, 124, 127, 144
Wachowski, Lana and Lila, 87
Wallace, Matt, 188
Watson, Emma, 10
Willcocks, Daniel, 187-188
Williams, Maisie, 9
willingness, 11, 25-33, 57, 73, 79, 94, 117, 127, 132, 154-155, 180

word counts, 64, 66
writer's block, 1-3, 30, 39, 49, 125-129
Writer's Market, 77, 90, 176
writing sprint, 66
writing yourself into a corner, 54, 66, 80, 84
YouTube, 61, 127, 132, 189

About the Author

Dharma Kelleher writes gritty crime thrillers including the Jinx Ballou Bounty Hunter series and the Shea Stevens Outlaw Biker series.

She is one of the only openly transgender authors in the crime fiction genre. Her action-driven thrillers explore the complexities of social and criminal justice in a world where the legal system favors the privileged.

Dharma is a member of Sisters in Crime, the International Thriller Writers, and the Alliance of Independent Authors.

She lives in Arizona with her wife and a black cat named Mouse. Learn more about Dharma and her work at https://dharmakelleher.com.